Conquer New Standards

Literary Text

Table of Contents

Introduction

Many states have adopted standards that set clear expectations about what students need to learn at each grade level. The standards are designed to be rigorous and pertinent to the real world, and they reflect the knowledge and skills that our young people need for success in college and careers.

Why *Conquer New Standards: Literary Text*?
As a teacher, you are required to incorporate these standards into your lesson plans. Your students may need targeted practice in order to meet grade-level standards and be promoted to the next grade.

Conquer New Standards: Literary Text provides you with ready-to-go units that support students in the development of key skills outlined in the standards (see the chart on page 5). Each unit includes one or more passages as well as a model of a response to a question about that passage. After reading the passage and reviewing the model, students practice applying the modeled skill by answering a variety of questions, including constructed response and multiple choice.

> **This book is appropriate for on-grade-level students as well as for English Learners and those requiring intervention.**

Many state standards have these key expectations:	In *Conquer New Standards: Literary Text*, students will:
Students must read a "staircase" of increasingly complex texts in order to be ready for the demands of college and career-level reading.	• Read passages independently. • Encounter a range of complex passages.
Students must read a diverse array of classic and contemporary literature from around the world. Students must come to understand other perspectives and cultures.	• Read classic literature. • Read contemporary literature. • Read about a wide diversity of characters and cultures, as well as stories from around the world. • Read a variety of genres: fiction, poetry, drama, myths, and more.
Students must show a "steadily growing ability" to comprehend and analyze text.	• Engage in a focused review of specific text comprehension skills. • Develop their understanding of each skill through modeled examples. • Encounter assessment items in each unit that tests the unit skill as well as skills reviewed earlier in the book.
Students must respond critically to three main text types: opinion/argument, informational, and narrative.	• Read a variety of narrative texts and have multiple opportunities to develop responses.
Students must engage effectively in a range of collaborative discussions (one-on-one, in groups, and teacher-led) with diverse partners on appropriate topics and texts, building on others' ideas and expressing their own clearly.	• Discuss skills and engage in skill-focused activities with teachers, peers, and parents/guardians to extend their understandings of skills.
Students must use multimedia resources.	• Encounter texts with intricate illustrations, such as a graphic novel. • Participate in guided multimedia activities.
Students must value evidence.	• Answer a wide array of assessment questions, both multiple choice and open ended, using evidence gathered from supplied passages to support their responses.

The companion book, *Conquer New Standards: Informational Text*, offers students opportunities to respond to opinion/argument and informational texts.

What You'll Find in This Book

This book offers skill-specific units with appealing texts and assessment-style questions, discussion prompts to further student understanding, and activities—all of which can be used in the classroom for independent work or as homework assignments. When used as homework, the units are a great way to foster a home-school connection. The materials in this book are also great for small- and whole-group lessons. See page 11 for suggestions about how to use the units in a variety of settings.

The Units

Each unit begins with either a single text or a pair of texts.

> Before assigning the first unit for students to do independently, model how to read—and reread—a passage.
>
> 1. Think about the purpose for reading the passage.
> 2. Read the passage all the way through to get the gist of it.
> 3. Reread the passage again, more slowly.
> 4. Refer to the passage to answer the questions.

Target Skill
Each unit includes a target skill that students will review and practice throughout the unit.

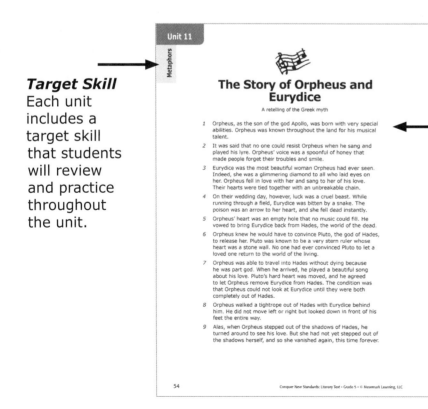

On-Level Texts
All of the texts have been created to offer grade-appropriate reading experiences for students. Students should read the passages independently. Avoid front-loading information or pre-teaching vocabulary. This will provide students with practice similar to the assessments they will eventually take.

Modeling and Tips

Each unit provides a page with a brief review of the skill along with a sample question, an explanation of the sample answer, and an additional opportunity for students to apply their learning at home.

Review the Skill

This section provides a focused description of the unit's skill as a helpful reminder to students.

Home-School Connection

A Home-School Connection activity is provided in each unit. It provides a brief activity for parents and guardians to build on what students are learning in school. The activity is focused on the unit skill and involves everyday materials.

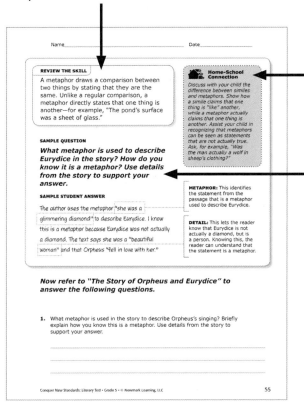

Sample Question and Sample Answer

Each unit offers a sample question focused on the unit skill followed by a sample student answer. Clues guide students to better understand how the sample answer uses text evidence to accurately and comprehensively answer the sample question. This section of each unit models how to read, answer, and provide text support with an assessment-style question, so that students are better prepared to answer questions independently.

Independent Practice

Each unit provides a variety of assessment-style questions. Students will encounter multiple-choice questions with single correct answers, multiple-choice questions with several correct answers, two-part questions, and open-ended questions requiring them to write short, constructed responses. These questions give students opportunities to apply their understanding of the unit skill and show their comprehension of the unit text. Students can work through these items independently to become experienced assessment takers.

Constructed-Response Questions

Multiple-Choice Questions

Two-Part Questions

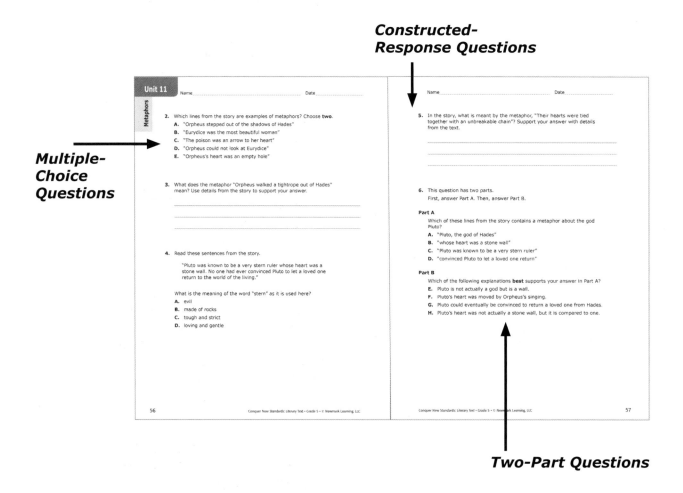

Conquer New Standards: Literary Text • Grade 5 • © Newmark Learning, LLC

Discuss and Share

At the back of the book, you will find additional resources to support students in becoming successful readers. Sentence starters are provided for each unit to make it easy to encourage further discussion of unit texts and skills. Additional at-home activities can be used to help students and their families build greater real-world connections and a deeper understanding of the reading skills.

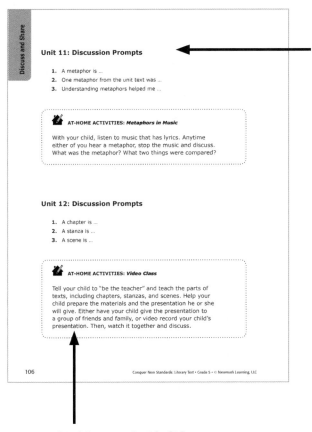

Discussion Prompts
Encourage students to talk about the skills they just reviewed. Through discussion, students can identify areas of confusion, build on each other's thoughts, and phrase skills in their own words. These prompts can be used either in the classroom, in small-group and whole-group settings, or at home to encourage a deeper consideration of important reading comprehension skills.

At-Home Activities
For each unit, there is a quick activity focused on the skill. These activities provide kinesthetic, auditory, visual, and cooperative learning experiences.

Answer Key

Each book contains an answer key that includes rationales and sample answers. Teachers may choose to:

- Review students' responses themselves.
- Assign students to review their own responses or work with a partner to review each other's responses.
- Send the answer key home so that parents or guardians can review students' responses.

Answer Key

4. Sample answer: The author of "An Emerald Is As Green As Grass" used similes to describe how interesting the colors of different gems are. The descriptions "An emerald is as green as grass" and a ruby is "red as blood" both show readers in vivid ways how these stones look. These are both similes because they use "as" to show comparisons.

5. **Part A**   C

    Part B   G   The author of "An Emerald Is As Green As Grass" most likely used this simile as a way to contrast sapphires with flint. The next line describes a flint, stating, "A flint lies in the mud." This shows a contrast to the line about sapphires. Additionally, the end of the poem mentions a flint again. In reading the entire poem, we see it is meant to show that stones like emeralds and sapphires may be beautiful and flint may not be beautiful, but flint is still very important.

6. Sample answer: The author of "A Red, Red Rose" wrote "O my Luve's like the melodie, / That's sweetly play'd in tune." I know this is a simile because of the words "like the" before the word "melodie." I think the word "melodie" is the same as "melody" because he says it is "sweetly play'd in tune." This simile tells us that the speaker's "Luve" is similar to a sweet melody, which means that she is very sweet and lovely.

Unit 11
pages 54–57

1. Sample answer: The line "Orpheus's voice was a spoonful of honey" is a metaphor used to describe Orpheus's singing. It's a metaphor because it states that his voice was something else, not just that it was "like" something else. Orpheus's voice was not actually a spoonful of honey. The metaphor is used to show that Orpheus had a very pleasing voice.

2. **C, E** The question asks readers to find more metaphors in the passage. Answer choices C and E are examples of metaphors because they describe one thing by naming it as a different thing.

3. Sample answer: This metaphor compares Orpheus's path out of Hades to a tightrope. The metaphor means that Orpheus walked very straight and very carefully, just like a performer on a tightrope. He did not actually walk on a tightrope but walked carefully so he would not turn or stumble. The text says he "did not move left or right but looked down in front of his feet the entire way."

4. **C** The question asks readers to define the word "stern" as it is used in the passage. In this context, the word "stern" means "tough and strict." Pluto is described as having a heart that is a "stone wall" and as never letting "a loved one return to the world of the living." These details tell the reader that Pluto was not someone who was easy to bargain with.

Sample Answer

The sample answer provides an ideal example of a written response, which can be used to evaluate students' written responses as well as provide students with ideas for improving their written responses.

Rationale

The rationale provides further explanation about the question and the unit skill, which can help students who had difficulties with a question.

How to Use *Conquer New Standards: Literary Text*

This book has been designed so that students can work independently—either in class or at home—making it easy for you to reinforce standards mastery without sacrificing valuable teaching time. But the units also work well for small- and whole-group lessons. The chart below outlines some ideas for incorporating the units into your teaching.

If you want to use this book ENTIRELY for classroom work:		
Units	Answer Key	Discuss and Share
Assign students to work on the units independently in class.	Review students' work using the answer key, OR allow students to grade their own work with the answer key.	Use the discussion prompts to lead small-group or whole-group discussions. Use the activities as opportunities for independent, partnered, small-group, or whole-group experiences.

If you want to use this book for a COMBINATION of classroom work and homework:		
Units	Answer Key	Discuss and Share
Assign students to work on the units independently in class.	Review students' work using the answer key, OR allow students to grade their own work with the answer key.	Use the discussion prompts to lead small-group or whole-group discussions.
		Copy the activities and send home as homework opportunities for the student to complete with a parent or guardian.

If you want to use this book ENTIRELY for homework:		
Units	Answer Key	Discuss and Share
Copy the Parent/Guardian Letter and units and send home for students to do as homework.	Photocopy the answer key for students, parents, or guardians to use to review the students' work.	Copy the discussion prompts and activities to send home as homework, encouraging parental/guardian involvement.

Dear Parent or Guardian,

This year, your child will be completing literary text units for homework. The goal of these units is to ensure that your child has the skills necessary to comprehend a variety of key literary text types, such as stories, poems, fables, folk tales, and plays.

There are three parts in the take-home unit:
1) the literary text passage;
2) a review of the skill being addressed that includes a sample question and sample answer about the text; and
3) questions about the passage for your child to answer

Encourage your child to read each passage independently if possible, and then review the skill and the sample question and answer. Finally, have him or her answer the unit questions.

The unit also includes engaging activities for you to do with your child at home to further support his or her understanding.

We hope you'll agree that the skills practice that *Conquer New Standards: Literary Text* offers will not only help your child to become a better reader, but also provide him or her with the support needed to become a more successful student.

Estimados padres o tutores:

La tarea de su hija(o) para este año consiste en leer y practicar ejercicios de unidades de textos literarios. El objetivo de estas unidades es garantizar que su hija(o) posea las destrezas necesarias para entender una amplia variedad de textos literarios como cuentos, poemas, fábulas, cuentos populares y obras dramáticas.

La unidad de la tarea en casa consta de tres partes:
1) el pasaje de texto literario;
2) un repaso de la destreza a desarrollar, que incluye ejemplos de pregunta y respuesta sobre el texto;
3) preguntas acerca del pasaje para que su hija(o) las responda

Anime a su hija(o) a leer cada pasaje de manera independiente, si es posible. Después, repase la destreza y los ejemplos de pregunta y respuesta. Para terminar, pídale que responda las preguntas de la unidad.

La unidad también incluye entretenidas actividades para que las hagan juntos en casa. Esto apoyará aún más la habilidad de comprensión de su hija(o).

Confiamos en que estará de acuerdo que la práctica de destrezas que ofrece *Conquer New Standards: Literary Text,* ayudará a su hija(o) a ser mejor lector(a) y, además, le brinda el apoyo necesario para ser un(a) estudiante de éxito.

Silent Storm

1   After months of classes, I was ready to make my first solo sailing trip. Before we get to that, though, there's something you should probably know: I'm deaf. My teachers were worried when I insisted on making a solo sail like my classmates, but my parents stuck up for me. "He's a great sailor," they told my instructors.

2   There is nothing better than wind rustling my hair and ocean spray dampening my T-shirt. *I am so ready for this,* I thought. Here I was at last, sailing solo. The ocean spread out before me like a clean sheet across my bed.

3   Soon, though, a dark cloud loomed on the horizon. I couldn't see anything ahead, let alone my destination, an island owned by my sailing school with a picnic area and a surprise treat prepared for me. But I'd sailed in storms before, and I knew to read the wind by watching the telltales, little ribbons of fabric attached to the sail. I knew to pay attention to every tiny detail.

4   Suddenly the wind was a gale pelting my face with brutally cold raindrops. Then out of nowhere, it changed directions, blowing the sail straight into my side and knocking me down. I could see the mainline of the sail from where I was and knew I had to let it out or the boat would capsize.

5   But I was too late—my boat capsized, and waves covered my head as I struggled to breathe. My boat was upside down and drifting farther and farther away. But I knew what to do. I had to climb on top of the boat and carefully push the far end of the boat until the mast came out of the water.

6   After a few tries, I finally flipped the boat. And as fast as the storm started, it ended; soon I was sailing in the sun. When I reached the island, I was so excited: a pitcher of fresh orange juice, all for me, was waiting.

     Conquer New Standards: Literary Text • Grade 5 • © Newmark Learning, LLC

REVIEW THE SKILL

To answer questions about a story, think about what each question is asking you. Then look back at the text for details that tell you the answer. Quoting directly from the text will support your answer.

Home-School Connection

Help your child understand that it is important to use the text to answer questions about a story. Even when asked to make inferences about the meaning of a text, the text itself will provide clues. Read a story with your child and ask questions that will require him or her to go back to the text. Ask your child to read aloud specific quotes in response to your questions.

SAMPLE QUESTION

What are two things that the narrator enjoys about sailing? Quote specific details from the text to support your answer.

SAMPLE STUDENT ANSWER

The narrator says, "There is nothing better than wind rustling my hair and ocean spray dampening my T-shirt." Because he says there is "nothing better," it is clear that these are two things he loves.

DETAIL 1: This detail describes one specific thing that happens while he's sailing.

DETAIL 2: This detail explains how he feels about the two specific things he mentions.

Now refer to "Silent Storm" to answer the following questions.

1. Why might the narrator's teachers be worried about him making a solo sail? Quote specific information from the story in your response.

_____

_____

_____

2. What are the steps the narrator had to take to get his boat upright after it capsized? Pick **two** steps that are stated in the text.

    A. He had to watch the telltales.

    B. He had to climb on top of the boat.

    C. He had to let the mainline out of the sail.

    D. He had to feel the wind blowing in his face.

    E. He had to carefully push the far end of the boat until the mast came out.

3. Read the sentence from the story. Then answer the question.

    "I couldn't see anything ahead, let alone my destination, an island owned by my sailing school with a picnic area and a surprise treat prepared for me."

    What is the meaning of the word "destination?"

    A. a picnic area

    B. a surprise treat

    C. a sailing school

    D. a place where someone is going

4. Review these quotes from the story. In what order did these events occur? Put them in order by writing a number from 1 to 5 in each blank next to an event.

    A. _____ "I finally flipped the boat."

    B. _____ "my parents stuck up for me."

    C. _____ "my boat capsized, and waves covered my head"

    D. _____ "Soon, though, a dark cloud loomed on the horizon."

    E. _____ "The ocean spread out before me like a clean sheet across my bed."

5. This question has two parts.

First, answer Part A. Then, answer Part B.

Part A

The narrator thinks, "I am so ready for this." What is he ready for?

- **A.** He is ready to read the telltales.
- **B.** He is ready to sail to the island alone.
- **C.** He is ready to drink fresh orange juice.
- **D.** He is ready to capsize his boat on purpose.

Part B

Which statements from the story directly support your answer to Part A? Choose **two**.

- **E.** "But I knew what to do."
- **F.** "My teachers were worried when I insisted"
- **G.** "I could see the mainline of the sail from where I was"
- **H.** "But I'd sailed in storms before, and I knew to read the wind"
- **I.** "Suddenly the wind was a gale pelting my face with brutally cold raindrops."

6. Read this sentence from the passage.

"'He's a great sailor,' they told my instructors."

Explain why the narrator's parents would believe that he is a great sailor. Quote details from the story to support your answer.

_____

_____

_____

Golden Baby

1   Whenever she could get away from her grandma and baby brother, Louisa crept silently into her grandma's room and raided her jewelry box. Louisa had dolled herself up with as many rings and necklaces and bracelets as she could find. She was sparkling like a house decked out for the holidays when her grandma came into the room and grabbed her hand.

2   "Where did you find this ring?" Grandma demanded. "This isn't your ring, and you had no right!"

3   "Grandma, I … I," Louisa stumbled. "It was in this little velvet bag at the bottom of your jewelry box, just like everything else in there." Grandma pulled the ring off Louisa's finger and shoved it in her pocket, then she turned and left the room.

4   That night, after her mom got home from work, Louisa asked about the ring.

5   "Oh, that was probably Bébé Or," her mother said. "Bébé Or is French for 'gold baby.' Your grandma has had Bébé Or forever, but she never told me where she got it."

6   Louisa was confused: Who would name a ring and then not even talk about it? If a thing had a name, she thought, then it must be important—and important things had stories. And there was no better place to find a story than in the boxes up in the attic.

7   The next morning, Louisa snuck like a thief up the attic steps and started blowing dust off boxes. In an old, yellowing photo album, she discovered a photograph of a man and a woman holding hands. The woman was wearing Bébé Or.

8   Louisa bucked up her courage, went downstairs, and asked her grandmother about the picture.

9   "Oh, Louisa, that's your grandfather and I," Grandma said wistfully. Louisa was shocked. "He went off to fight in the Korean War and never came back. That's why I was so upset yesterday seeing that ring—it still hurts to think of losing him."

10 Louisa smiled at her grandmother. "He looks like a perfect gentleman, Grandma," she said.

REVIEW THE SKILL

To draw inferences, you draw conclusions about things the author did not state directly by combining clues from the text with what you already know about the world.

 Home-School Connection

Remind your child that the text itself will provide clues for making inferences. Help your child practice making inferences by reading a book together. Pose questions that require him or her to point to clues in the text about things not stated directly. Discuss ways that your child can combine these clues with what he or she already knows in order to understand important ideas.

SAMPLE QUESTION

What inference can you draw about the fact that Grandma got upset with Louisa? Use details from the story to support your response.

SAMPLE STUDENT ANSWER

I think that the ring Grandma pulls off Louisa's finger and shoves in her pocket must be more special than the other jewelry Louisa is wearing. Grandma doesn't seem to mind that Louisa is "sparkling like a house decked out for the holidays." This tells me that this ring is different from all the other pieces of jewelry. It must mean something special to Grandma.

DETAIL 1: This detail shows an important action that Grandma takes.

DETAIL 2: This detail gives a clue that Grandma might feel differently about this ring than about the other pieces of jewelry. It allows readers to draw the inference that this particular ring is special.

Now refer to "Golden Baby" to answer the following questions.

1. Why might Louisa be confused by Grandma's reaction to one ring of many that she is wearing? Use details from the story to support your answer.

_____

_____

_____

Name_____ Date_____

2. What two inferences can the reader make based on Grandma's overall reaction to Louisa wearing Bébé Or? Pick the **two** inferences that are most reasonable.

   A. Grandma thinks the ring is dangerous.

   B. Grandma doesn't want to talk about the ring.

   C. Grandma is excited that Louisa found the ring.

   D. Grandma has a strong emotional attachment to the ring.

   E. Grandma doesn't want Louisa to play with any of her jewelry.

3. Read the sentence from the story. Then answer the question.

   "'Grandma, I … I,' Louisa stumbled."

   What is the meaning of the word "stumbled" in this sentence?

   A. to hit your foot on something while walking and fall

   B. to make mistakes or hesitate in speech

   C. to discover something accidentally

   D. to walk unsteadily

4. Read the sentence from the story. Then answer the question.

   "The next morning, Louisa snuck like a thief up the attic steps and started blowing dust off boxes."

   Why would Louisa have to sneak up to the attic? Use details from the story to support your answer.

   _____

   _____

   _____

5. This question has two parts.

First, answer Part A. Then, answer Part B.

Part A

Read these sentences from the text.

"'Oh, Louisa, that's your grandfather and I,' Grandma said wistfully. Louisa was shocked."

What is the most reasonable inference you can make about why Louisa would be shocked?

A. Louisa didn't think her grandmother liked wearing rings.

B. Grandma had never talked to Louisa about her grandfather.

C. The people in the photo didn't look like a grandmother and grandfather.

D. Louisa's mother had told Louisa there were no photos of her grandmother.

Part B

Which quote from the story **best** supports your answer in Part A?

E. "This isn't your ring, and you had no right!"

F. "He looks like a perfect gentleman, Grandma."

G. "He went off to fight in the Korean War and never came back."

H. "Your grandma has had Bébé Or forever, but she never told me where she got it."

6. What inference can you make about the relationship between Louisa and Grandma from the end of the story? Use details from the story to support your answer.

_____

_____

_____

The Lion and the Hunter

On the grassy green veld,
a lion with a mane like a sunflower
lies still and humbled.

King of the pride no more,
5   his limbs are limp and his head
heavy as an anvil.

There is no glory here,
not for the man with the gun
kneeling over the lion

10 and not for the lion,
whose tawny body
will never prowl the veld

again. The veld falls silent,
quiet as a grave, and the hunter
15 smiles a grin like a sneer.

Months later, in the hunter's
den, the lion stands,
mane combed and eyes glassy.

Instead of blood pumping
20 through muscles, he is wool
stretched over wires.

Instead of tremendous and
fearsome, he is posed
and contained. Wild no more.

REVIEW THE SKILL

The theme of a text is its main idea or underlying meaning. It is an overarching idea that the author is trying to convey to you through the text.

Home-School Connection

Remind your child that finding the theme requires having a grasp of the entirety of a text. Strong readers will be able to hang onto the overall theme of a text while using specific text examples to help support that theme. Help your child practice identifying themes by discussing a favorite movie. Ask your child to describe what he or she thinks the main message or idea of the movie is.

SAMPLE QUESTION

How do the descriptions of the lion in the first two stanzas begin to introduce the poem's theme? Use details from the poem to support your answer.

SAMPLE STUDENT ANSWER

The poem begins with positive phrases "mane like a sunflower" and "King of the pride" to talk about the lion. Then the poem states that the lion is "still and humbled" and his head is "heavy as an anvil." These are sad images. So the first two stanzas suggest a theme about something great becoming something sad.

CLUE 1: These details are positive descriptions that convey beauty and power.

CLUE 2: These details paint much gloomier images.

Now refer to "The Lion and the Hunter" to answer the following questions.

1. How does the title suggest the poem's theme? Use details from the poem to support your answer.

_____

_____

_____

Name_____ Date_____

2. Read these lines from the poem. Then answer the question.

"Instead of tremendous and / fearsome, he is posed / and contained."

What is the meaning of the word "tremendous" in this sentence?
A. enormous in size and power
B. very easily embarrassed
C. shaking with fear
D. poisonous

3. What descriptions of the lion when it was alive support the poem's theme? Pick **three** choices.
A. "blood pumping through muscles"
B. "mane combed and eyes glassy"
C. "tremendous and fearsome"
D. "tawny"
E. "silent"

4. Reread lines 7–10. Explain what the speaker thinks of the hunter and his actions. Use details from the poem to support your answer.

_____

_____

_____

5. This question has two parts.

First, answer Part A. Then, answer Part B.

Part A

Which sentence would be **best** to include in an explanation of the poem's theme?

A. The hunter and the lion should have left each other alone.

B. The hunter took something beautiful and ruined it.

C. The hunter was right to kill and stuff the lion.

D. The hunter had no choice but to kill the lion.

Part B

Which phrase from the poem **best** supports your answer in Part A?

E. "the lion stands, mane combed"

F. "tremendous and fearsome"

G. "On the grassy green veld"

H. "There is no glory here"

6. What is the theme of the poem? Use details from the text to support your answer.

_____

_____

_____

The Splits

1   It had always been this way—Robert sleeping on his bed in his half of the room and me on my bed in my half of the room. A few years ago we painted my half of the room bright green and his half a tasteful dark blue. It was a "compromise," as my mom said, but Robert and I both loved how we could share the room but still have our own space.

2   All of a sudden, yesterday morning, Robert sat down to his bowl of oatmeal and said, "Christiane, it's time we moved into separate rooms. I'm too grown up for our current, childish arrangement."

3   Well, you could have knocked me over with a feather, I was so stunned. There he was, in his cartoon mouse pajamas, telling me he was too grown up for me?

4   Before I even had a chance to reply, Mom said, "You know, Christiane, maybe Robert's right. Maybe it's time we turn the guest room into your bedroom."

5   "Mom, that is so unfair!" I cried. "Why do I have to be the one to move when this wasn't even my idea?" I pouted and left my oatmeal on the table to grow as cold as my broken heart.

6   "Christiane, sis, you know it's not that I don't want to be with you, right?" Robert said, looking at me sincerely. I ignored him and got ready for school in silence.

7   After school, I was working on my splits at gymnastics practice. Gradually, I worked my way lower and lower, stretching my legs ever further. "Splits," I said to myself. "Maybe I need to think of moving out of the bedroom the same way I think about these splits. It's going to hurt at first, but then I'll get used to it. And we'll both have extra room to stretch out."

8   At home, I gave Robert a hug and said, "I get it, bro. I'll help you repaint your room if you help me repaint my new one."

REVIEW THE SKILL

A summary is a short recounting of a body of text. You can summarize a paragraph, a page, or an entire text. A summary should include the important events that occurred in the text and any important details that help another reader understand the key events.

Home-School Connection

Strong readers will be able to summarize what they have read, showing that they have deeply understood the most important details. Read a story along with your child, pausing after every paragraph and taking turns summarizing the most important details from each paragraph.

SAMPLE QUESTION

Read the first paragraph. How would a reader summarize the information in this paragraph?

SAMPLE STUDENT ANSWER

The narrator and her brother, Robert, were splitting a room, with her side painted green and his side painted blue. They loved sharing a room together.

CLUE 1: This is the main idea of the paragraph. This idea should be included in a summary of the paragraph.

CLUE 2: This is an important detail that supports the main idea of the paragraph.

Now refer to "The Splits" to answer the following questions.

1. What happens in the second paragraph? Use details from the story to summarize this paragraph.

_____

_____

_____

Name_____ Date_____

2. Reread paragraphs 3–5. Which of the following details would you include in a summary of these paragraphs? Choose **two**.

   A. Christiane is surprised by Robert's statement.

   B. Robert was wearing "cartoon mouse pajamas."

   C. Christiane leaves her oatmeal on the table to grow cold.

   D. Mom speaks before Christiane has a chance to answer Robert.

   E. Christiane thinks it's unfair that she should be the one to move.

3. Read the sentences from the story. Then answer the question.

   "Well, you could have knocked me over with a feather, I was so stunned. There he was, in his cartoon mouse pajamas, telling me he was too grown up for me?"

   What is the meaning of the word "stunned" in this sentence?

   A. extremely surprised

   B. shocked with electricity

   C. excited about a new idea

   D. knocked unconscious from a blow

4. Put the following events from the passage in the order in which they happen. Write a number from 1 to 5 in each blank next to an event.

   A. _____ Christiane notices the similarity between doing the splits and her brother's idea.

   B. _____ Christiane ignores Robert's explanation and gets ready for school in silence.

   C. _____ Mom suggests that they turn the guest room into Christiane's room.

   D. _____ Robert decides that he and Christiane need to have separate rooms.

   E. _____ Christiane offers to help Robert paint his new room.

5. This question has two parts.

First, answer Part A. Then, answer Part B.

Part A

Which sentence **best** summarizes paragraph 7?

- **A.** While practicing splits, Christiane decides that they are too hard to do, much like moving out of her room.
- **B.** While practicing splits, Christiane decides to tell Robert that she can no longer participate in gymnastics.
- **C.** While practicing splits, Christiane realizes that, even though moving will hurt, it will be better in the end.
- **D.** While practicing splits, Christiane realizes that Robert should be the one to move out of their room.

Part B

Which sentence from the text **best** supports your answer in Part A?

- **E.** "It's going to hurt at first, but then I'll get used to it."
- **F.** "'I'm too grown up for our current, childish arrangement.'"
- **G.** "'Why do I have to be the one to move when this wasn't even my idea?'"
- **H.** "'Christiane, sis, you know it's not that I don't want to be with you, right?'"

6. Write a summary of the story "The Splits." Remember to only include the most important details.

_____

_____

_____

How Bear Lost His Tail

adapted from the Iroquois myth

1   A long time ago, Bear had a beautiful, long, furry tail that he loved to show off. Everyone thought Bear was very vain about his tail, but they were frightened of his big claws.

2   One chilly day, Bear went lumbering down to the lake. Fox was relaxing on the ice, surrounded by fish. She knew that Bear was hungry, and she decided to trick him to teach him a lesson.

3   Fox greeted Bear, and when Bear asked where the fish came from, Fox told him she had caught them. Bear was shocked, since Fox didn't have any fishing tools. "I caught them using my tail," Fox told Bear. "It's really the best tool for catching fish."

4   Fox offered to show Bear how it worked. She accompanied Bear to another part of the lake, and Bear cut a hole in the ice with his claws. Fox told Bear to drop his tail into the water, and she assured him that he would feel it when a fish bit him. "When you pull your tail out, there will be a fish at the end of it," Fox said, "but it's very important that you sit very still and think only about fish."

5   Because Bear was so vain about his tail, he was confident that he could catch more fish than any other animal could. "I'll watch from the trees at the lake's edge so that I don't scare the fish," Fox told Bear. Instead, though, Fox took her fish home, and Bear fell asleep.

6   A few hours later, Fox returned. She snuck up on the sleeping bear and shouted, "A fish! I see a fish on your tail!" Bear quickly woke up and felt a sharp pain in his frozen tail. He leaped up, and his tail snapped off; all that was left was a small stump where his beautiful tail had been. Bear was furious, but Fox ran off giggling—and this is why bears have short tails and are not friends with foxes to this day.

REVIEW THE SKILL

All the elements of a story work together. Characters are the people or animals in the story. The setting, or settings, is where and when the story takes place. The events are the things that happen in the story. All of these elements help a story make sense.

Home-School Connection

Strong readers take note of each element of a story during the course of reading. To help your child develop the skill of describing characters, settings, and events in detail, discuss one of his or her favorite books together. Ask your child about the details that describe the various story elements in the book and how these elements work together.

SAMPLE QUESTION

Give one detail that describes each character in the story. Use information from the text to support your answer.

SAMPLE STUDENT ANSWER

In the first paragraph of the story, the text says, "Everyone thought Bear was very vain about his tail" and that Bear "loved to show off" his tail. This lets us know that Bear thinks a lot of himself and his tail. In the second paragraph, the text says that Fox "decided to trick" Bear, so I think she likes to play tricks.

DETAIL 1: This detail describes Bear. It gives the important information that Bear thinks very highly of himself.

DETAIL 2: This detail gives the reader information about Fox. Because Fox decided to trick Bear, a reader can infer that Fox likes to play tricks on others.

Now refer to "How Bear Lost His Tail" to answer the following questions.

1. Where and when do the events in the story take place? Use details from the story in your answer.

_____

_____

_____

Name_____ Date_____

2. What are **two** things Fox does in order to trick Bear?
   A. She runs off giggling.
   B. She relaxes on the ice.
   C. She thinks Bear is very vain.
   D. She sneaks up on Bear after he falls asleep.
   E. She tells Bear to drop his tail into the water.
   F. She makes sure that Bear will never again go hungry.

3. Read the sentence from the story. Then answer the question.

   "Bear was furious, but Fox ran off giggling—and this is why
   bears have short tails and are not friends with foxes to this
   day."

   What is the meaning of the word "furious" in this sentence?
   A. very energetic
   B. wild with speed
   C. extremely angry
   D. like an intense storm

4. According to the story, why was Bear confident that he could catch more
   fish than any other animal?
   A. He thought very hard about fish while he sat fishing.
   B. He cut a hole in the ice with his own claws.
   C. He had brought his own tools for fishing.
   D. He was very vain.

5. This question has two parts.

First, answer Part A. Then, answer Part B.

Part A

The last paragraph states that "Fox ran off giggling." Why was Fox giggling?

- **A.** She was pleased that she had tricked Bear.
- **B.** She had succeeded in making Bear her enemy.
- **C.** She was happy that she had taught Bear how to fish.
- **D.** She had wanted Bear to lose his tail because she was jealous of it.

Part B

Which sentence from the story **best** supports your answer in Part A?

- **E.** "Fox offered to show Bear how it worked."
- **F.** "Bear was shocked, since Fox didn't have any fishing tools."
- **G.** "Bear quickly woke up and felt a sharp pain in his frozen tail."
- **H.** "Everyone thought Bear was very vain about his tail, but they were frightened of his big claws."

6. How do the characters, setting, and events work together to tell the story of Bear losing his tail? Be sure to give details from the story to support your answer.

_____

_____

_____

Adapted and excerpted from
Peter Pan

By J. M. Barrie

1   There was another light in the room now, a thousand times brighter than the night-lights. It was not really a light; it made this light by flashing so quickly, but when it came to rest for a second you saw it was a fairy, a girl called Tinker Bell.

2   A moment after the fairy's entrance the window was blown open by the breathing of the little stars, and Peter dropped in. He had carried Tinker Bell part of the way, and his hand was still messy with the fairy dust.

3   "Tinker Bell," he called softly, after making sure that the children were asleep. "Tink, where are you?" She was in a jug for the moment, and liking it extremely; she had never been in a jug before.

4   "Oh, do come out of that jug, and tell me, do you know where they put my shadow?"

5   The loveliest tinkle as of golden bells answered him. It is the fairy language. You ordinary children can never hear it, but if you were to hear it you would know that you had heard it once before.

6   Tink said that the shadow was in the big box. She meant the chest of drawers, and Peter jumped at the drawers, scattering their contents to the floor with both hands. In a moment he had recovered his shadow, and in his delight he forgot that he had shut Tinker Bell up in the drawer.

7   If he thought at all, but I don't believe he ever thought, it was that he and his shadow, when brought near each other, would join like drops of water, and when they did not he was appalled.

8   He tried to stick it on with soap from the bathroom, but that also failed. A shudder passed through Peter, and he sat on the floor and cried.

9   His sobs woke Wendy, and she sat up in bed.

10   "My name is Wendy Moira Angela Darling," she said with some satisfaction. "What is your name?"

11   "Peter Pan."

REVIEW THE SKILL

To compare two or more things means to explain how they are the same. To contrast two or more things means to tell how they are different. When reading stories, compare and contrast different characters.

 Home-School Connection

Decide on a favorite book with your child and ask him or her to tell you about the book's different characters. Ask, "How are they alike? How are they different? How do their qualities affect the story?" Strong readers will be able to apply this same approach when reading new stories.

SAMPLE QUESTION

What is one way that Peter Pan and Tinker Bell are alike? Use details from the text to support your answer.

SAMPLE STUDENT ANSWER

Peter Pan and Tinker Bell are alike because neither one is a regular person. In the first paragraph, Tinker Bell is described as "a fairy." In the fourth paragraph, Peter asks Tinker Bell, "do you know where they put my shadow?" This tells us that Peter's shadow is not attached to him anymore. These details about Tinker Bell and Peter tell us they are not regular people.

DETAIL 1: The reader is told that there was "a fairy" named Tinker Bell. Since a fairy is a magical creature, the reader knows that Tinker Bell is not a regular person.

DETAIL 2: This text tells the reader that somehow Peter Pan and his shadow have been separated. This is not something that happens in real life, so the reader can infer that Peter Pan is also a magical creature of some kind.

Now refer to excerpt adapted from Peter Pan *to answer the following questions.*

1. Why is Peter Pan in this room? Use details from the text to support your answer.

_____

_____

_____

2. Which phrase from the story describes Tinker Bell's language? Use details from the text to find your answer.

   A. "a thousand times brighter than the night-lights"

   B. "The loveliest tinkle as of golden bells"

   C. "the breathing of the little stars"

   D. "messy with the fairy dust"

3. Which details from the story support the idea that Peter Pan and Tinker Bell are different? Pick **two** choices.

   A. Peter Pan cares about finding his shadow.

   B. Peter Pan can understand the fairy language.

   C. Tinker Bell entered the room through the window.

   D. Other people can understand Peter Pan when he speaks.

   E. Tinker Bell is small enough for Peter Pan to carry in his hand.

4. Read these sentences from the story.

   > "She meant the chest of drawers, and Peter jumped at the drawers, scattering their contents to the floor with both hands. In a moment he had recovered his shadow, and in his delight he forgot that he had shut Tinker Bell up in the drawer."

   What is the meaning of the word "recovered?"

   A. lost

   B. remembered

   C. got back again

   D. covered up again

5. This question has two parts.

First, answer Part A. Then, answer Part B.

Part A

According to the text, how does Peter Pan behave toward Tinker Bell?

- **A.** He is thankful to her for helping him find his shadow.
- **B.** He is angry with her for leaving fairy dust on his hand.
- **C.** He is a little thoughtless and not very grateful for her help.
- **D.** He is bossy because he makes her look for his shadow alone and won't help.

Part B

Which detail from the text **best** supports your answer in Part A?

- **E.** Peter Pan jumps toward the chest of drawers.
- **F.** Peter Pan throws what was in the drawers on the floor.
- **G.** Tinker Bell tells Peter Pan that his shadow is in the big box.
- **H.** After Peter Pan finds his shadow, he forgets that Tinker Bell is in a drawer.

6. Based on the text, how are Peter and Tinker Bell alike and how are they different? Be sure to give details from the story to support your answer.

_____

_____

_____

The New Place

1   *This is it,* Bea thought. The day she had been dreading had arrived, and now she was in line with her family to board the vessel that would take them to their new home, Nova Loko. It would be a long trip, since they had to leave their solar system. She turned and took one last long look at the only planet she had ever known, Earth.

2   Bea remembered the news reports that announced that Earth would become uninhabitable, even though she had only been 5 years old. Even then, the air had been painful to breathe. The planet had become too polluted and too hot, and the weather had changed so quickly that the trees could not adapt. They lost their leaves for the last time that autumn. The following spring, there were no crocuses to announce warm weather. The landscape had changed from white and gray to brown and gray, and the search for a new planet had begun seriously.

3   The survey team had gotten lucky. Only two years after they started looking, they found a planet that seemed promising. The next year, the exploration crew landed on Nova Loko safely. When they sent back pictures of the landscape, no one could believe that the sky on Nova Loko was green and not blue. There were lakes, but only in perfect circles. Trees had no branches—they stood straight up and down like telephone poles. Long red stems covered the ground instead of grass. But the planet was clean, the air was healthy, and it was a safe distance from a sun.

4   *I think I can make this work,* Bea thought. It would be a little cooler—even at the equator, the new planet's temperature would only rise to 65 degrees Fahrenheit. She would learn to love wearing sweaters, she decided. She had prepared herself for four years. It was time for something new, as difficult and scary as it might be. She held on to her parents' hands and walked onto the spaceship.

REVIEW THE SKILL

The setting of a story is where and when the story takes place. The setting can play an important part in a character's actions or feelings. To compare and contrast different settings is to note how they are alike and different and how they might be important to the story.

Home-School Connection

Help your child practice comparing and contrasting settings by first discussing what settings are in a particular story. Choose a favorite book together. The settings might be obvious. For example, different paragraphs might describe different settings. But if the settings are not obvious, point out words that have to do with a landscape or particular place (such as sky or land). Strong readers will be able to find important descriptive words to keep in mind as they compare and contrast settings.

SAMPLE QUESTION

What is one description the author gives of the first planet, and one description the author gives of the second planet? Support your answer with details from the text.

SAMPLE STUDENT ANSWER

One description the author gives about Earth is that "the air had been painful to breathe." One description the author gives about Nova Loko is that "Long red stems covered the ground."

DETAIL 1: This detail is used to describe Earth.

DETAIL 2: This detail is used to describe Nova Loko.

Now refer to "The New Place" to answer the following questions.

1. Why did the news reports, mentioned in paragraph 2, say that Earth will become uninhabitable? Use details from the story to support your answer.

_____

_____

_____

Name_____ Date_____

2. Which details show how Nova Loko is different from Earth? Pick **two** choices.

   A. It had a colored sky.

   B. It was a safe distance from a sun.

   C. Its lakes only formed in perfect circles.

   D. Its landscape had become brown and gray.

   E. Its trees stood straight up and down like telephone poles.

3. Read the sentences from the story. Then answer the question.

   > "The survey team had gotten lucky. Only two years after they started looking, they found a planet that seemed promising."

   What is the meaning of the word "survey" as used in the passage?

   A. a collection of soil from a planet

   B. a list of questions a person answers

   C. a special sport played only in outer space

   D. a close examination of something in order to figure out its value

4. Which of the following is true of both Earth and Nova Loko?

   A. The temperature on the planet rises to only 65 degrees.

   B. The planet's ground is covered with long red stems.

   C. The air on the planet is painful to breathe.

   D. The planet is a safe distance from a sun.

5. This question has two parts.

First, answer Part A. Then, answer Part B.

Part A

In the last paragraph, Bea thinks, "I think I can make this work." What is she referring to?

A. She thinks she can figure out how to regrow the trees' leaves.

B. She thinks she can learn more about Nova Loko before deciding to move.

C. She thinks she can keep living in her original setting, Earth, and fix the environment.

D. She thinks she can accept her change of setting and embrace the move to Nova Loko.

Part B

Which statement from the text **best** supports your answer in Part A?

E. "and the search for a new planet had begun seriously"

F. "It was time for something new, as difficult and scary as it might be."

G. "No one could believe that the sky on Nova Loko was green and not blue"

H. "She turned and took one last long look at the only planet she had ever known, Earth."

6. Explain how the two planets in the story are alike and how they are different. How do their characteristics affect the story? Give details from the story to support your answer.

_____

_____

_____

Yusef on Track

1   Yusef was not having the kind of season he had hoped for. When he started running track in the fall, he had felt unbeatable—and Coach Margaret was impressed. "You could be the best distance runner in town," she told Yusef during an early chat. Yusef's first two meets had felt more like practice than competition. He easily beat the other boys in his first 1,600-meter race. His second race was even easier: By the time he passed the finish line, only one other racer was even on the same lap. He had begun to feel he could be great at this.

2   But as Yusef went to more meets, he met other kids from middle schools twice as big as his. These kids had been running for longer, and they were *fast.* In his third and fourth races, Yusef struggled to keep up with the winners. He even had to sprint to stay on the lead lap during his fourth race. He only placed third because the boy in front of him sprained his ankle making a turn on his final lap. It struck Yusef that maybe he wasn't as talented as he had thought.

3   Yusef went to Coach Margaret and tried to quit. "You can quit if you want to," she said, "but I still think you can be the fastest distance runner in town—if you're willing to work at it." Yusef took her words to heart. He decided that if his coach believed in him, he should believe in himself too. That day he started lifting weights with his legs and learning a longer stride.

4   At the last meet of the season, Yusef raced like he was born to run. He shocked the boy who was expected to win when he breezed right past him with a lap to go. When his shoes zipped across the finish line, Yusef made a time that was better than anyone else's all season. *This is what confidence feels like*, he thought with a smile.

 Conquer New Standards: Literary Text • Grade 5 • © Newmark Learning, LLC

REVIEW THE SKILL

The events in a story are the things that happen. Pay special attention to a story's different events and how they are alike and different. Often, how a character in a story responds to a series of events is important to the character's development.

Home-School Connection

To help your child practice comparing and contrasting events in a story, consider a pair of recent events from his or her own life—for example, the last two birthday parties attended or the last two sports events he or she participated in. Ask your child to discuss similarities and differences between these events and how he or she was affected by or responded to the different events.

SAMPLE QUESTION

Compare and contrast Yusef's first two races. Use details from the story to support your answer.

SAMPLE STUDENT ANSWER

Yusef's first two races were alike because he won both of them easily. The text says his first two meets "had felt more like practice than competition" to him. The races were different, though, because the second race "was even easier" than the first. The text says that "only one other racer was even on the same lap" when Yusef finished the second race.

DETAIL 1: This detail supports the idea that Yusef's first two races were alike because they were both very easy for him.

DETAIL 2: This detail shows a way that Yusef's second race was different from the first. It supports the idea that the second race was even easier than the first one.

Now refer to "Yusef on Track" to answer the following questions.

1. How were Yusef's first two races the same as and different from his second two races? Use details from the story to support your answer.

_____

_____

_____

Name_____ Date_____

2. After several races, Yusef felt that "maybe he wasn't as talented as he had thought." Which of these events made him feel this way? Choose **two**.

   A. the first two meets, which felt more like practice than competition

   B. his third and fourth races, in which he struggled to keep up with the winners

   C. his second race, in which there was one other racer on the same lap at the end

   D. his fourth race, in which he placed third only because another runner was injured

   E. a conversation with his coach, in which she said he could be the best distance runner in town

3. Read these sentences from the story. Then answer the question.

   "He decided that if his coach believed in him, he should believe in himself too. That day he started lifting weights with his legs and learning a longer stride."

   What is the meaning of "stride" as it is used in the story?

   A. an impatient walk

   B. a step forward in progress

   C. a regular pace while running or walking

   D. a point where one reaches the best version of himself or herself

4. In what ways were Yusef's two conversations with his coach **similar**? In what ways were they **different**? Use details from the text in your answer.

   _____

   _____

   _____

5. This question has two parts.

First, answer Part A. Then, answer Part B.

Part A

How did Yusef's second conversation with his coach affect his thinking?

   A. He decided he was going to quit running.

   B. He decided to work harder to become better.

   C. He decided his third and fourth races wouldn't be important.

   D. He decided that he could be great at running the 1,600-meter race.

Part B

Which statement from the story **best** supports your answer choice in Part A?

   E. "He had begun to feel he could be great at this."

   F. "It struck Yusef that maybe he wasn't as talented as he had thought."

   G. "At the last meet of the season, Yusef raced like he was born to run."

   H. "That day he started lifting weights with his legs and learning a longer stride."

6. How did the different events in the story affect Yusef's development as a character? Use details from the story to support your answer.

_____

_____

_____

The Emperor's New Clothes

1   A long time ago, in the land of Denmark, there was a very vain king. He cared for nothing more than his wardrobe. He was always buying the finest clothes, and filling the rooms of his castles as if they were closets. But no matter how many fine shirts, trousers, and robes he collected, he was never satisfied.

2   The king began hiring the most skilled tailors in the land to make clothing for him. He bought the finest materials for them to work with, and treated them as honored guests. The tailors he hired were given servants of their own to accommodate any needs they might have.

3   Three strangers came before the king one day, with an extraordinary claim. They boasted of a cloth they could weave from enchanted wool and gold. They said this cloth could be used to fashion a set of clothes finer and more beautiful than any worn by man or king. They further promised that this clothing would be invisible to any foolish man who was not competent for his position.

4   The king was captivated by this report. He would have the finest clothes in the land. He would also always know if his advisers were smart and trustworthy at their jobs. He quickly ordered that the three strangers be afforded every luxury in the castle. The strangers got to work immediately.

5   Night and day, the strangers pretended to weave these fantastic clothes. None of the king's advisers would admit that they saw nothing being made. They did not want to admit the clothes were invisible to them.

6   When the clothes were finished, the king remarked on their beauty. He asked each of his advisers if they had ever seen finer clothes. Everyone agreed. He paid the strangers handsomely, and paraded throughout the kingdom for all to see.

7   When an innocent young boy said the king wasn't wearing anything, the embarrassed king realized he had been duped.

REVIEW THE SKILL

Passages and stories may contain unfamiliar words you do not know. You can look at how the word is used in a sentence to find its meaning. Other descriptions in the passage, or context clues, can help you determine what the word might mean.

 Home-School Connection

Read a book with your child and encourage your child to point out any unfamiliar words. Help your child determine the meaning of each word using context clues in the text. Then make up several additional sentences that use the word in context. Show your child how the use of the word can reveal its meaning. For more difficult words, encourage your child to use a dictionary to find the most likely meaning of the word.

SAMPLE QUESTION

What is the meaning of the word "wardrobe" as it is used in the story? Use details from the story to support your answer.

SAMPLE STUDENT ANSWER

The word "wardrobe" in this story seems to mean "a collection of clothes". The passage talks about how the king "cared for nothing more than his wardrobe," and then it talks about all the clothes the king had and how he kept "filling the rooms of his castle as if they were closets."

MEANING: This identifies the meaning of the word "wardrobe."

CONTEXT CLUES: These context clues support the idea that a "wardrobe" refers to the entire collection of clothes the king has.

Now refer to "The Emperor's New Clothes" to answer the following questions.

1. What does the word "captivated" mean as it is used in the story? Use details from the story to support your answer.

_____

_____

_____

Name_____ Date_____

2. Read the sentence from the passage. Then answer the question.

   "The king began hiring the most skilled tailors in the land to make clothing for him."

   Based on the context of the sentence, what is the **most precise** meaning of "tailors"? Use details from the text to support your answer.

   _____

   _____

   _____

3. Which detail from the story tell the reader that the three strangers did not actually make any clothes at all? Choose **two**.

   A. "the king remarked on their beauty."

   B. "The king was captivated by this report."

   C. "the embarrassed king realized he had been duped"

   D. "this cloth could be used to fashion a set of clothes"

   E. "the strangers pretended to weave these fantastic clothes"

4. Which of the following has a meaning **similar** to the word "duped" as it is used in the story?

   A. naked

   B. tricked

   C. laughed at

   D. well rewarded

5. What is the meaning of the word "fashion" as it is used in the story?

   A. the latest style

   B. make

   C. buy

   D. see

6. This question has two parts.

  First answer Part A. Then answer Part B.

Part A

What does the word "competent" mean as it is used in the story?

   A. paid well

   B. old enough

   C. well trained

   D. willing to agree

Part B

Which of the following statements **best** supports your answer in Part A?

   E. The king was willing to pay any price for fine clothing.

   F. The king himself thought the clothes were very beautiful.

   G. The king wanted to know which of his men were not good at their jobs.

   H. The king was shown the truth by a young person, not the men who worked for him.

A Red, Red Rose

By Robert Burns

O my Luve's like a red, red rose,
That's newly sprung in June:
O my Luve's like the melodie,
That's sweetly play'd in tune.

5   As fair art thou, my bonie lass,
So deep in luve am I;
And I will luve thee still, my dear,
Till a' the seas gang dry.

Till a' the seas gang dry, my dear,
10   And the rocks melt wi' the sun;
And I will luve thee still, my dear,
While the sands o' life shall run.

And fare-thee-weel, my only Luve!
And fare-thee-weel, a while!
15   And I will come again, my Luve,
Tho' 'twere ten thousand mile!

An Emerald Is As Green As Grass

By Christina Rossetti

An emerald is as green as grass;
   A ruby red as blood;
A sapphire shines as blue as heaven;
   A flint lies in the mud.
5   A diamond is a brilliant stone,
   To catch the world's desire;
An opal holds a fiery spark;
   But a flint holds fire.

Name_____ Date_____

REVIEW THE SKILL

A simile compares two things in a certain way. A simile usually uses the words "as" or "like" to show a way in which one thing is similar to a very different thing. "Her hair was as smooth as silk" and "he slept like a log" are examples of similes.

Home-School Connection

Discuss similes with your child. Begin by sharing with your child common phrases and clichés that use similes. Guide your child to identify the comparison being made between the two things. Then ask him or her to determine several ways in which the two things being compared are alike and not alike.

SAMPLE QUESTION

In "A Red, Red Rose," the speaker compares the woman he loves to a rose. In what way does he believe they are similar? Use details from the poem to support your answer.

SAMPLE STUDENT ANSWER

In "A Red, Red Rose," the speaker says his "Luve" is "like a red, red rose" because she is lovely and beautiful, like a new rose. We can infer this because he uses the words "That's newly sprung in June" to describe the rose. He is describing a rose that has just bloomed, so we can imagine it is very beautiful.

SIMILE: These are the key words that show that a comparison is being made using a simile.

DETAIL: This detail supports the idea that both the speaker's "Luve" and the rose are very lovely and beautiful.

Now refer to "A Red, Red Rose" and "An Emerald Is As Green As Grass" to answer the following questions.

1. In the poem "An Emerald Is As Green As Grass," there are many examples of similes. Choose one simile and explain what makes it a simile and what items are being compared.

_____

_____

_____

Similes

2. Read these lines from the poem "A Red, Red Rose."

"As fair art thou, my bonie lass, / So deep in luve am I;"

What does the word "fair" mean as it is used in this poem?

   A. beautiful

   B. honest

   C. light colored

   D. similar

3. Which lines from the poem "An Emerald Is As Green As Grass" are examples of **similes**? Choose **two**.

   A. "A ruby red as blood;"

   B. "But a flint holds fire."

   C. "To catch the world's desire;"

   D. "An opal holds a fiery spark;"

   E. "A diamond is a brilliant stone,"

   F. "A sapphire shines as blue as heaven;"

4. How did the author of "An Emerald Is As Green As Grass" use similes to describe different stones and gems? Use details from the poem to support your answer.

_____

_____

_____

5. This question has two parts.

First, answer Part A. Then, answer Part B.

Part A

Which of the following is most likely the reason the author used the simile "A sapphire shines as blue as heaven" in the poem "An Emerald Is As Green As Grass"?

  A. to describe the exact color of a sapphire

  B. to show how heaven and Earth are similar

  C. to show a difference between a sapphire and a flint

  D. to explain to readers that sapphires are the most beautiful gems in the poem

Part B

Which of the following explanations **best** supports your answer in Part A?

  E. This line is the longest line of the poem.

  F. The next line of the poem describes what mud is.

  G. The next line in the poem says "A flint lies in the mud."

  H. Each line of the poem describes a different kind of gem or stone.

6. Explain how the author of "A Red, Red Rose" used a simile to compare his "Luve" to a song. Use details from the poem to support your answer.

_____

_____

_____

The Story of Orpheus and Eurydice

a retelling of the Greek myth

1   Orpheus, as the son of the god Apollo, was born with very special abilities. Orpheus was known throughout the land for his musical talent.

2   It was said that no one could resist Orpheus when he sang and played his lyre. Orpheus's voice was a spoonful of honey that made people forget their troubles and smile.

3   Eurydice was the most beautiful woman Orpheus had ever seen. Indeed, she was a glimmering diamond to all who laid eyes on her. Orpheus fell in love with her and sang to her of his love. Their hearts were tied together with an unbreakable chain.

4   On their wedding day, however, luck was a cruel beast. While running through a field, Eurydice was bitten by a snake. The poison was an arrow to her heart, and she fell dead instantly.

5   Orpheus's heart was an empty hole that no music could fill. He vowed to bring Eurydice back from Hades, the world of the dead.

6   Orpheus knew he would have to convince Pluto, the god of Hades, to release her. Pluto was known to be a very stern ruler whose heart was a stone wall. No one had ever convinced Pluto to let a loved one return to the world of the living.

7   Orpheus was able to travel into Hades without dying because he was part god. When he arrived, he played a beautiful song about his love. Pluto's hard heart was moved, and he agreed to let Orpheus remove Eurydice from Hades. The condition was that Orpheus could not look at Eurydice until they were both completely out of Hades.

8   Orpheus walked a tightrope out of Hades with Eurydice behind him. He did not move left or right but looked down in front of his feet the entire way.

9   Alas, when Orpheus stepped out of the shadows of Hades, he turned around to see his love. But she had not yet stepped out of the shadows herself, and so she vanished again, this time forever.

Name_____ Date_____

REVIEW THE SKILL

A metaphor draws a comparison between two things by stating that they are the same. Unlike a regular comparison, a metaphor directly states that one thing is another—for example, "The pond's surface was a sheet of glass."

Home-School Connection

Discuss with your child the difference between similes and metaphors. Show how a simile claims that one thing is "like" another, while a metaphor actually claims that one thing is another. Assist your child in recognizing that metaphors can be seen as statements that are not actually true. Ask, for example, "Was the man actually a wolf in sheep's clothing?"

SAMPLE QUESTION

What metaphor is used to describe Eurydice in the story? How do you know it is a metaphor? Use details from the story to support your answer.

SAMPLE STUDENT ANSWER

The author uses the metaphor "she was a glimmering diamond" to describe Eurydice. I know this is a metaphor because Eurydice was not actually a diamond. The text says she was a "beautiful woman" and that Orpheus "fell in love with her."

METAPHOR: This identifies the statement from the passage that is a metaphor used to describe Eurydice.

DETAIL: This lets the reader know that Eurydice is not actually a diamond, but is a person. Knowing this, the reader can understand that the statement is a metaphor.

Now refer to "The Story of Orpheus and Eurydice" to answer the following questions.

1. What metaphor is used in the story to describe Orpheus's singing? Briefly explain how you know this is a metaphor. Use details from the story to support your answer.

_____

_____

_____

Name_____ Date_____

2. Which lines from the story are examples of metaphors? Choose **two**.

   A. "Orpheus stepped out of the shadows of Hades"

   B. "Eurydice was the most beautiful woman"

   C. "The poison was an arrow to her heart"

   D. "Orpheus could not look at Eurydice"

   E. "Orpheus's heart was an empty hole"

3. What does the metaphor "Orpheus walked a tightrope out of Hades" mean? Use details from the story to support your answer.

   _____

   _____

   _____

4. Read these sentences from the story.

   "Pluto was known to be a very stern ruler whose heart was a stone wall. No one had ever convinced Pluto to let a loved one return to the world of the living."

   What is the meaning of the word "stern" as it is used here?

   A. evil

   B. made of rocks

   C. tough and strict

   D. loving and gentle

Name_____ Date_____

5. In the story, what is meant by the metaphor, "Their hearts were tied together with an unbreakable chain"? Support your answer with details from the text.

_____

_____

_____

6. This question has two parts.

First, answer Part A. Then, answer Part B.

Part A

Which of these lines from the story contains a metaphor about the god Pluto?

   A. "Pluto, the god of Hades"

   B. "whose heart was a stone wall"

   C. "Pluto was known to be a very stern ruler"

   D. "convinced Pluto to let a loved one return"

Part B

Which of the following explanations **best** supports your answer in Part A?

   E. Pluto is not actually a god but is a wall.

   F. Pluto's heart was moved by Orpheus's singing.

   G. Pluto could eventually be convinced to return a loved one from Hades.

   H. Pluto's heart was not actually a stone wall, but it is compared to one.

Fruits Throughout the Year

In the spring, we sing! We look for the sun,
and we watch for the buds to bloom.
We stain our lips with strawberries for fun
and are thrilled to get out of our rooms.

5   In summer, we sweat and hurry to the shade
to eat our watermelon in peace.
Bees and ants get shooed away,
and we can never just eat one piece.

The days start to shrink when autumn descends,
10 and the apples start to fall from their trees.
The sound of a crunch marks the warm weather's end,
and we wear pants that will cover our knees.

When winter's first snow hits the ground then we know
that fruit eating is going to get tough.
15 We buy oranges from Florida and bananas from Mexico,
and hunker down in the North's icy rough.

We eat fruit all through the year.
Some days it comes from just down the street.
But whether the fruit comes from far or from near,
20 its sweet taste is always a treat!

Conquer New Standards: Literary Text • Grade 5 • © Newmark Learning, LLC

REVIEW THE SKILL

All types of text are structured. For example, fiction is structured in paragraphs and chapters. Poems contain lines and stanzas. Dramas and plays contain scenes.

Home-School Connection

Read aloud to your child, while pointing out and naming the parts of the text—such as chapter, unit, stanza, scene, introduction, and conclusion. Then have your child find examples of the parts of text and name them in several different books.

SAMPLE QUESTION

Which stanza is about fruit that you can eat in the summer? Use details from the poem to support your answer.

SAMPLE STUDENT ANSWER

As I read the poem, I noticed the second stanza mentions the word "summer" in the first line. Then in the second line, I see the word "watermelon," so the second stanza is about summer fruits, specifically watermelon.

DETAIL 1: The second stanza mentions summer, so this detail supports the answer.

DETAIL 2: The second stanza talks about eating watermelon. Watermelon must be a fruit you can eat in the summer. This detail also supports the answer.

Now refer to "Fruits Throughout the Year" to answer the following questions.

1. How is the fifth stanza different from all the other stanzas? Use details from the poem to support your answer.

_____

_____

_____

2. Which stanza is about fruit in the autumn?

    A. stanza 2

    B. stanza 3

    C. stanza 4

    D. stanza 5

3. What is the most likely reason the author starts the poem with a stanza about fruit in spring? Choose the **two** most reasonable answers.

    A. The author wanted to start with the warmest season.

    B. The author wanted to use the season that has the most fruit.

    C. The author wanted to start with the season most people like the best.

    D. The author wanted to set up the poem's structure of pairing a fruit with a season.

    E. The author wanted to start the poem with spring because it is the season at the beginning of the year.

4. Read these lines from the poem. Then answer the question.

> The days start to shrink when autumn descends, / and the apples start to fall from their trees. / The sound of a crunch marks the warm weather's end, / and we wear pants that will cover our knees.

In this stanza, what is the meaning of the word "crunch?"

    A. a noisy action

    B. a dangerous situation

    C. something you need

    D. pushing things together

5. This question has two parts.

First, answer Part A. Then, answer Part B.

Part A

The poem describes eating fruit. How does the act of eating fruit change from stanza 3 to stanza 4?

A. The fruit tastes bad.

B. There is no fruit to eat.

C. Eating fruit gets easier.

D. Eating fruit gets harder.

Part B

Which line from the text **best** supports your answer in Part A?

E. "and we wear pants that will cover our knees"

F. "and the apples start to fall from their trees"

G. "and hunker down in the North's icy rough"

H. "that fruit eating is going to get tough"

6. Based on the details in the poem, how would you describe the speaker of the poem? Use details from the poem to support your answer.

_____

_____

_____

Kamilah, PI

1   It was 3:05 p.m. when Nolan shuffled into the library. I had been sitting there quietly, doing my homework.

2   "Um," he started. I glanced up, and as soon as I saw the sadness in his face, I knew my homework was not going to be done this afternoon.

3   Nolan was the tallest kid in fifth grade; he was so tall he seemed practically like a tree when he stood by my table. But as tall as he was, he didn't say much, and it was generally established that he tried very hard to be invisible (and succeeded most of the time). I was pretty sure this was the first time he had ever approached me with what seemed like even an attempt at speaking.

4   This is not to say that he was the first kid to ever approach me. My classmates regarded me as someone who could help. I could get things done and solve problems. It's true most people can help another person out, but for some reason, I was just better at it than most. I was both proud of and a little embarrassed by this remarkable reputation.

5   I didn't help everyone who asked, since it really depended on the type of favor or issue, but I heard everyone out; and if I thought someone really needed help, I'd do my best to solve his or her problem and crack the case.

6   My name is Kamilah, but everyone calls me "K." They also call me the "PI"—private investigator. I'm class vice president (being president takes up too much free time), and I play clarinet badly. I don't look for problems, but they seem to find me, which was why I feared it would be a long afternoon.

7   "What can I do for you, Nolan?" I asked in a tone I thought appropriate.

8   "I need your help to find my dog," he whimpered, looking like he might crumble.

Name_____ Date_____

 Home-School Connection

Remind your child that strong readers are always thinking about how each part of a text relates to the larger text and how each piece fits into the whole, like a puzzle. Help your child reread the beginning of a favorite book and talk about how the beginning works to build the story.

SAMPLE QUESTION

Reread the first sentence of the story. How does it start to build the story? Use details from the text to support your answer.

SAMPLE STUDENT ANSWER

When I reread the first sentence, the first thing I see is that it's 3:05 in the afternoon, so I know the story won't be taking place during school hours. The second part of the sentence talks about Nolan as he "shuffled into the library." "Shuffled" doesn't show excitement or happiness. I don't think Nolan is happy.

CLUE 1: The first sentence tells what time of day the story is taking place. It begins to build the setting.

CLUE 2: Because Nolan is mentioned right away, it's likely that he will be one of the main characters. The description of his walk begins to tell readers what he is like and how he is feeling.

Now refer to "Kamilah, PI" to answer the following questions.

1. This is the beginning of what kind of story? Use details from the text in your answer.

_____

_____

_____

2. Reread the third paragraph. What are **two** qualities that Kamilah notes about Nolan?

   A. Nolan is very tall.

   B. Nolan is very outgoing and social.

   C. Nolan knows how to solve problems.

   D. Nolan does not generally approach people and talk.

   E. Nolan has special powers that let him turn invisible.

3. Read these sentences from the story.

   "This is not to say that he was the first kid to ever approach me. My classmates regarded me as someone who could help. ... I was both proud of and a little embarrassed by this remarkable reputation."

   In this paragraph, what is the meaning of the word "reputation?"

   A. the level of respect others have for a person

   B. a state of being well known for acting badly

   C. a dangerous situation

   D. an act of heroism

4. Reread the fourth paragraph. What is Kamilah's reputation?

   A. She is too lazy to be class president.

   B. She helps everyone who asks for it.

   C. She doesn't like Nolan.

   D. She can fix problems.

5. This question has two parts.

First, answer Part A. Then, answer Part B.

Part A

Based on the text's structure and what you've learned about Kamilah, what will be the **most likely** outcome of her meeting with Nolan?

   A. She will refuse to help Nolan because she doesn't like dogs.

   B. She will tell Nolan to find a teacher to help him.

   C. She will meet Nolan after her clarinet practice.

   D. She will help Nolan solve his problem.

Part B

Which quote from the text **best** supports your answer in Part A?

   E. "I feared it would be a long afternoon."

   F. "it really depended on the type of favor or issue"

   G. "It was 3:05 when Nolan shuffled into the library."

   H. "It's true most people can help another person out"

6. Based on the text, is it likely that Kamilah will be able to help Nolan? Why or why not? Support your answer with details from the text.

_____

_____

_____

Adapted and excerpted from
Heidi

By Johanna Spyri

1   Heidi immediately recognized Clara's handwriting, and bounding over to her grandfather, and exclaimed: "A letter has come from Clara. Wouldn't you like me to read it to you, grandfather?"

2   Heidi immediately read to her two listeners, as follows.

3   Dear Heidi:

4   We are all packed up and shall travel in two or three days. Papa is leaving, too, but not with us, for he has to go to Paris first. The dear doctor visits us now every day, and as soon as he opens the door, he calls, "Away to the Alps!" for he can hardly wait for us to go. If you only knew how he enjoyed being with you last fall! He came nearly every day this winter to tell us all about you and the grandfather and the mountains and the flowers he saw. He said that it was so quiet in the pure, delicious air, away from towns and streets, that everybody has to get well there. He is much better himself since his visit, and seems younger and happier. Oh, how I look forward to it all! The doctor's advice is, that I shall go to Ragatz first for about six weeks, then I can go to live in the village, and from there I shall come to see you every fine day. Grandmama, who is coming with me, is looking forward to the trip too. But just think, Miss Rottenmeier does not want to go. When grandmama urges her, she always declines politely. I think Sebastian must have given her such a terrible description of the high rocks and fearful abysses, that she is afraid. I think he told her that it was not safe for anybody, and that only goats could climb such dreadful heights. She used to be so eager to go to Switzerland, but now neither she nor Tinette want to take the risk. I can hardly wait to see you again!

5   Good-bye, dear Heidi, with much love from grandmama,

6   I am your true friend,

7   Clara

REVIEW THE SKILL

Point of view is the narrator's perspective. In first person point of view, the character uses words like "I," "me," or "my." Third person point of view uses words like "he," "she," and "they."

Home-School Connection

Help your child practice describing point of view by reading together. Ask your child to tell about the narrator or main characters of each story. Then ask your child to determine the feelings, beliefs, and point of view of the characters by looking for clues in their words or their actions. Make sure your child pays close attention to positive or negative words used by the narrator or characters.

SAMPLE QUESTION

What conclusion can be drawn about Clara's point of view of Heidi? Use key details from the passage to support and explain your answer.

SAMPLE STUDENT ANSWER

Clara views Heidi in a happy, friendly way. She is excited to see her friend Heidi. You can tell because in her letter, Clara tells Heidi, "I can hardly wait to see you again!" This shows she is happy and excited to see Heidi. She also closes her letter by saying, "I am your true friend," which shows that Clara likes Heidi and considers her a friend.

POINT OF VIEW: This clearly states Clara's point of view of Heidi.

DETAILS: These statements provide supporting details that reveal how Clara is happy and excited about seeing her friend Heidi.

Now refer to the excerpt adapted from Heidi *to answer the following questions.*

1. Based on the passage, what inference can be made about the doctor's point of view of the Alps? Use key details from the passage to support and explain your answer.

_____

_____

_____

Name_____ Date_____

2. Read this sentence from the passage.

"When grandmama urges her, she always declines politely."

What is the **most precise** meaning of "declines?"
A. fails
B. lessens
C. refuses
D. suffers

3. This question has two parts.

First answer Part A. Then answer Part B.

Part A

What inference about Clara is supported by the story?
A. Clara does not enjoy traveling without her father.
B. Clara has never met Heidi or her grandfather before.
C. Clara is not well and is going on the trip to get better.
D. Clara is sad Miss Rottenmeier is not coming on the trip.

Part B

Which detail from the passage **best** supports your answer in Part A?
E. "He said that … everybody has to get well there."
F. "But just think, Miss Rottenmeier does not want to go."
G. "Papa is leaving, too, but not with us, for he has to go to Paris first."
H. "He came nearly every day this winter to tell us all about you and the grandfather"

4. Which of the following **best** reveal grandmama's point of view?
   Select **two** answers.
   - A. "I shall go to Ragatz first for about six weeks"
   - B. "She used to be so eager to go to Switzerland"
   - C. "but now neither Tinette nor she wants to take the risk"
   - D. "and that only goats could climb such dreadful heights"
   - E. "Good-bye, dear Heidi, with much love from grandmama"
   - F. "Grandmama, who is coming with me, is looking forward to the trip too."

5. What does the first paragraph show about Heidi's point of view?
   - A. Heidi wants to go away to visit Clara.
   - B. Heidi is excited to receive a letter from Clara.
   - C. Heidi is worried about reading the letter from Clara.
   - D. Heidi wants privacy while she reads the letter from Clara.

6. How does Clara's point of view differ from Miss Rottenmeier's point of view about the trip to the Alps? Use details from the story to support your answer.

   _____

   _____

   _____

Adapted and excerpted from
A Little Princess

By Frances Hodgson Burnett

1   "Here we are, Sara," said Captain Crewe, making his voice sound as cheerful as possible. Then he lifted her out of the cab and they mounted the steps and rang the bell. Sara often thought afterward that the house was somehow exactly like Miss Minchin. It was respectable and well furnished, but everything in it was ugly; and the very armchairs seemed to have hard bones in them. In the hall everything was hard and polished—even the red cheeks of the moon face on the tall clock in the corner had a severe varnished look. The drawing room into which they were ushered was covered by a carpet with a square pattern upon it; the chairs were square, and a heavy marble timepiece stood upon the heavy marble mantel.

2   As she sat down in one of the stiff mahogany chairs, Sara cast one of her quick looks about her.

3   "I don't like it, papa," she said. "But then I dare say soldiers— even brave ones—don't really LIKE going into battle."

4   Captain Crewe laughed outright at this. He was young and full of fun, and he never tired of hearing Sara's queer speeches.

5   "Oh, little Sara," he said. "What shall I do when I have no one to say solemn things to me? No one else is as solemn as you are."

6   "But why do solemn things make you laugh so?" inquired Sara.

7   "Because you are such fun when you say them," he answered, laughing still more. And then suddenly he swept her into his arms and kissed her very hard. He stopped laughing all at once and looked almost as if tears had come into his eyes.

8   It was just then that Miss Minchin entered the room. She was very like her house, Sara felt: tall and dull, and respectable and ugly. She had large, cold, fishy eyes, and a large, cold, fishy smile. It spread itself into a very large smile when she saw Sara and Captain Crewe.

REVIEW THE SKILL

Point of view is a term that describes the way that a narrator or character views events. Point of view is often expressed through descriptions, which influence how a reader thinks about events and characters in the story.

 Home-School Connection

Help your child practice describing how point of view influences descriptions in the text by reading a short story together. Have your child describe the point of view of the narrator. Then ask your child to identify descriptions in the story that reveal this point of view. Discuss how the narrator's point of view influenced the narrator's thoughts and feelings about the events and characters in the story.

SAMPLE QUESTION

What is Sara's point of view of Miss Minchin? Use key details from the passage to support your answer.

SAMPLE STUDENT ANSWER

Sara does not like Miss Minchin and thinks she is a mean person. I can tell Sara's point of view from the descriptions in the story. The story says that Sara thinks Miss Minchin is "tall and dull, and respectable and ugly." It also says that Sara thinks Miss Minchin has "large, cold, fishy eyes, and a large, cold, fishy smile." These details show Sara's point of view.

POINT OF VIEW: This statement describes Sara's point of view of Miss Minchin.

DESCRIPTIONS: These descriptions from the story support the answer about Sara's point of view.

Now refer to the excerpt adapted from A Little Princess to answer the following questions.

1. How does Sara's point of view influence the description of the house? Use details from the story to support your response.

    _____

    _____

    _____

Name_____ Date_____

2. Select **two** descriptions from the passage that show Sara's point of view in the story.

   A. "'I don't like it, papa,' she said."

   B. "She was very like her house, Sara felt: tall and dull"

   C. "It was just then that Miss Minchin entered the room."

   D. "'But why do solemn things make you laugh so?' inquired Sara."

   E. "Then he lifted her out of the cab and they mounted the steps and rang the bell."

   F. "the chairs were square, and a heavy marble timepiece stood upon the heavy marble mantel"

3. Read this sentence from the passage. Then answer the question.

   "In the hall everything was hard and polished—even the red cheeks of the moon face on the tall clock in the corner had a severe varnished look."

   Based on the context of the sentence, what is the **most precise** meaning of "severe?"

   A. detailed

   B. difficult

   C. important

   D. stern

4. Based on the passage, what inference can be made about Captain Crewe's feelings about leaving Sara? Use details from the passage to support and explain your answer.

   _____

   _____

   _____

5. This question has two parts.

First answer Part A. Then answer Part B.

Part A

Which of the following **best** describes Captain Crewe's point of view in the story?

    A. Captain Crewe feels he must hide his feelings to make Sara happy.

    B. Captain Crewe feels uncomfortable around Miss Minchin.

    C. Captain Crewe is happy to leave Sara with Miss Minchin.

    D. Captain Crewe is annoyed by Sara's solemn behavior.

Part B

Which sentence from the passage **best** supports your answer in Part A?

    E. "'But why do solemn things make you laugh so?' inquired Sara."

    F. "'What shall I do when I have no one to say solemn things to me?'"

    G. "It spread itself into a very large smile when she saw Sara and Captain Crewe."

    H. "'Here we are, Sara,' said Captain Crewe, making his voice sound as cheerful as possible."

6. Which sentence from the passage **best** supports the conclusion that Sara's father is leaving to fight in a war?

    A. "'But why do solemn things make you laugh so?' inquired Sara."

    B. "It spread itself into a very large smile when she saw Sara and Captain Crewe."

    C. "'But then I dare say soldiers—even brave ones—don't really LIKE going into battle.'"

    D. "'Because you are such fun when you say them,' he answered, laughing still more."

How Illustrations Contribute to Meaning

The Monster on the Mountain

adapted and excerpted from *Frankenstein* by Mary Wollstonecraft Shelley

REVIEW THE SKILL

Some texts you read have illustrations that go with them. Sometimes, the illustrations may be more important than the words. It is important to interpret the meanings of both the words and illustrations while reading fictional texts. If an author includes illustrations, try to determine how these illustrations affect the meaning.

Home-School Connection

Ask your child to discuss how a page of a graphic novel or other illustration-heavy text would be different without the illustrations. Read the text without showing your child the illustrations. Then have your child read the text while looking at the illustrations. Encourage your child to share whether he or she enjoyed the text more with or without the illustrations included and why. Ask your child to tell you what value the illustrations added to the story.

SAMPLE QUESTION

How do the illustrations affect the text that is provided in the graphic novel? Support your answer with details from the text.

SAMPLE STUDENT ANSWER

The author uses illustrations to show much of the action. There are less descriptions of the characters, setting, and action than text without illustrations because it is shown in the pictures.

DETAIL 1: This identifies the purpose of the illustrations.

DETAIL 2: This identifies that the illustrations take the place of descriptions in text.

Now refer to "The Monster on the Mountain" to answer the following questions.

1. In panel 2, how does the illustration help you understand the action more than the text alone? Use details from the text to support your answer.

_____

_____

_____

Name_____ Date_____

2. Which of the following **best** identifies the mood created by the illustrations in panel 1?

   A. hopefulness

   B. loneliness

   C. relaxation

   D. relief

3. How does the illustration in panel 5 help you understand the meaning behind the monster's words? Support your answer with details from the text.

   _____

   _____

   _____

4. Which ideas are supported by the illustration in panel 6? Choose **two.**

   A. Frankenstein agrees to talk with the monster.

   B. Frankenstein and the monster leave in different directions.

   C. Frankenstein and the monster continue to fight each other.

   D. The monster has prepared a place so that he and Frankenstein can speak.

   E. Frankenstein invites the monster to return to his castle and live with him.

5. What does the word "entreat" mean as it is used in the passage?

   A. beg

   B. favor

   C. leave

   D. punish

6. This question has two parts.

First answer Part A. Then answer Part B.

Part A

Which detail from the graphic novel do you know **only** because of the illustrations?

   A. The monster is able to communicate in English.

   B. The monster desperately wants to speak with Frankenstein.

   C. Frankenstein feels guilty that the monster is suffering.

   D. The monster is very large in comparison to Frankenstein.

Part B

Which of the following statements **best** supports your answer in Part A?

   E. Panel 5 shows the monster with a very angry face.

   F. Panel 4 shows the monster towering over Frankenstein.

   G. Panel 3 has an image of the monster on the mountain.

   H. Panel 4 has a speech bubble saying "I am your creature."

Adapted and excerpted from
Space Station 1

By Frank Belknap Long

Read the following passage silently, and then listen as your teacher or another adult reads it aloud.

1 The wound in his shoulder was no longer painless, but it had ceased to bleed profusely, and his exploring fingers convinced him that the knife had severed no more than a superficial ligament.

2 He still felt dizzy, and his head was aching a little, but he moved quickly through the darkness, his faculties heightened by an intensity of purpose, which enabled him to find the companionway without colliding with obstacles or taking a wrong turn. Up the stairway he climbed, still clutching the knife, prepared for a possible second encounter with its original owner...

3 "My God!" the Captain cried out, staring the hardest of all. "Where did you get that wound? Who attacked you? And what were you doing in my cabin?"

4 Corriston walked up to the Captain and said, in a voice that trembled a little, "May I talk to you privately, sir? What I have to say won't take long."

5 "Why not?" the Captain demanded. "That uniform you're wearing makes it mandatory. All right, come back into my cabin."

6 They went back into the cabin; the captain shut the door and turned to face Corriston with a shocked concern in his stare.

7 "You've had it rough, Lieutenant. I can see that."

8 "Plenty rough," Corriston conceded, "but it's not myself I'm worried about."

9 "Did you know that a man has just been wounded?"

10 "I know," Corriston said.

11 "With a poisoned barb, a Martian barb. It's a plant found only on Mars. We have him stretched out on a table in the sick bay now. Tell me something, Lieutenant. Did you just tangle with the man who did it?"

12 "I think so," Corriston said.

REVIEW THE SKILL

Multimedia can involve a variety of forms, such as the Internet, video, audio, and images. Encourage your child to consider how different forms present different details or highlight different meanings within a story.

 Home-School Connection

Offer your child additional multimedia options along with the unit story Space Station 1. For example, you could watch a science fiction movie together, clips from the NASA website about Mars, and more.

SAMPLE QUESTION

Did you feel differently about the Captain after hearing the passage read aloud? Use details from the text to support your response.

SAMPLE STUDENT ANSWER

When I read paragraph 3, I thought the Captain was angry at Corriston. The Captain said "what were you doing in my cabin?" and also "cried out." When I heard it read aloud, I thought the Captain might be taking Corriston's wound seriously and that might be why he "cried out" and asked questions.

READING: This detail is about the experience of reading paragraph 3.

HEARING: These details are about the experience of hearing paragraph 3 read aloud, and how this influenced the meaning of the story.

Now answer the following questions about your experience of both reading and listening to Space Station 1.

1. Describe one way the reading experience is different from the listening experience. Use details from the text to support your response.

_____

_____

_____

Name_____ Date_____

2. What does the word "superficial" mean as it is used in the passage?

   A. careless

   B. dangerous

   C. fake

   D. minor

3. Describe how listening versus reading affected your understanding of the conversation between the Captain and Corriston. Use details from the text to support your answer.

_____

_____

_____

4. This question has two parts.

First, answer Part A. Then, answer Part B.

Part A

How did Corriston get injured?

   A. He collided into something when walking in the dark.

   B. He was hurt by a dangerous Martian plant.

   C. He fought with someone who had a knife.

   D. He slipped while in the Captain's cabin.

Part B

Which detail from the text **best** supports your answer in Part A?

   E. "'With a poisoned barb, a Martian barb. It's a plant found only on Mars.'"

   F. "he moved quickly through the darkness, his faculties heightened"

   G. "the knife had severed no more than a superficial ligament"

   H. "'And what were you doing in my cabin?'"

5. Which of the following would you only be able to do when listening to someone read *Space Station 1* aloud? Select **two**.

   A. Picture what is going on in the story.

   B. Look back at earlier paragraphs to find a detail.

   C. Focus on how quickly or slowly a story is read.

   D. Reread a paragraph to better understand what is going on.

   E. Hear the way Corriston and the Captain might sound when they speak.

   F. Learn details about what the characters in *Space Station 1* look like.

6. How do multimedia elements, such as hearing the story read aloud or looking at the illustration below, help you understand the story? Use details from the story, the illustration, and the experience of listening to support your answer.

_____

_____

_____

Priya at the Office

By Danielle Martin

1   When my alarm clock rang that morning, I remembered my plans for the day. It was Take Your Daughter to Work Day, and I was spending the day with Mom at her office.

2   Normally, I'd be grateful for a day off from school without being sick, but not that day. We were studying states of matter in science class, so my teacher was making ice cream, and we were allowed to eat it in class. I was disappointed to miss my favorite treat, and my expectations for fun at Mom's office were low.

3   Mom and I arrived at the office at 8:30 a.m., and she began seeing patients promptly at 9 a.m. I wasn't invited into the exam rooms, but I watched the people as they shuffled in and out for their appointments. As the day continued, I was astonished at the significant role my mother played in people's lives!

4   "Priya, where are you?" Mom called down the hallway.

5   "Here, Mom," I responded from the waiting room.

6   "Please wait for me at my desk while I see another patient," she requested. "Then I have a surprise for you."

7   As I waited, I surveyed Mom's office. I noticed that the wall behind her desk was covered with thank-you cards. There were notes from men, women, children, and coworkers. More than one person wrote about how Mom helped improve their health—and their life in the process.

8   I was so absorbed in reading Mom's cards that I didn't hear her enter the room behind me.

9   "Are you ready to get some ice cream?" Mom asked.

10 "Mom, thanks for asking me to come here today," I said. "I never knew how important you are to others. You really make a difference in people's lives."

11 "Thank you, Priya," Mom said. "Helping people is the most important part of my job."

12 "Mom?" I said.

13 "Yes, Priya," Mom answered.

14 "Did I hear you say something about ice cream?" I said, and we both started laughing.

A Different Path

By Danielle Martin

1   With each passing birthday, Robert spent more time out on the farm with his father. Although he had been helping with household chores for a while, he used to have more freedom to fill his days with activities that actually interested him. Recently, his time was spent studying crops and milking dairy cows.

2   "Where are your thoughts, son?" Father's voice disturbed Robert's daydream. He was teaching Robert how to determine when the harvest was ready.

3   Robert answered quickly, "I am listening, Father," but Father had noticed his son's dissatisfaction for weeks now.

4   "You might not enjoy learning how to manage the farm, but this is important work," Father explained. "What work would you rather be doing right now?"

5   Robert did not have a simple answer, but he thought of Mother sewing because he enjoyed watching her take a few plain pieces of fabric and make them into something useful. He explained to Father: "I want to do what Mother does with fabric, but I do not want to sew clothes. It is difficult to explain."

6   Father listened carefully, nodded to express his understanding, and said, "You want to create useful objects with your own hands." Then he said, "Let us take a carriage ride, son."

7   Robert obeyed, and soon they arrived at a work shed with a strange sign out front. Robert could hear the echo of a hammer strike behind the door.

8   Father spoke: "Son, I have observed your disinterest in farming. It is fortunate that your older brother both enjoys and excels at it, so he will help me maintain the farm, and you will do better to take a different path."

9   "What different path, Father?" Robert inquired.

10 "Your Uncle John is the blacksmith here in Plymouth Colony," Father explained, "and I have arranged for you to learn about his trade. If you are interested, we can discuss when you will begin spending your days here."

11 "Perhaps tomorrow?" Robert suggested eagerly.

REVIEW THE SKILL

When comparing fiction, we think about how story elements are presented in different stories. Ask yourself, "How are they similar? How are they different?"

 Home-School Connection

Help your child practice comparing and contrasting by leading them to think about the similarities and differences between familiar people, objects, and situations. Use such conversation starters as "This reminds me of …" or "This is different from that time…" to model making connections.

SAMPLE QUESTION

Based on the titles of the two passages, predict whether their settings will be similar or different. Use details from both passages to support your response.

SAMPLE STUDENT ANSWER

Based on their titles, these two stories will probably have different settings. The word "office" in the title "Priya at the Office" suggests that the story is set in a city during more recent times. The word "path" in the title "A Different Path" suggests that this story is set in a more rural location.

CLUE 1: Readers can compare and contrast the ideas that keywords in the title represent. The keyword "office" is a clue that suggests a city setting for this story.

CLUE 2: The keyword "path" in "A Different Path" is a clue that suggests a country setting. Readers can contrast these ideas to predict that the stories will have different settings.

Now refer to "Priya at the Office" and "A Different Path" to answer the following questions.

1. Explain one theme that both "Priya at the Office" and "A Different Path" have in common. Use details from both passages to support your response.

_____

_____

_____

2. What is the meaning of the word "absorbed" in paragraph 8 of "Priya at the Office"?

    A. bored

    B. comfortable

    C. interested

    D. selfish

3. This question has two parts.

    First answer Part A. Then answer Part B.

Part A

Which statement correctly identifies a difference between the two passages?

    A. In "Priya at the Office," events are in the order they happened. In "A Different Path," events are presented through a series of memories.

    B. "Priya at the Office" uses dialogue between the characters. "A Different Path" uses narration to describe the characters' interactions.

    C. The first person narrator in "Priya at the Office" is Priya herself, while the third person narrator in "A Different Path" is not identified.

    D. The characters in "Priya at the Office" are a parent-child pair, while the characters in "A Different Path" are a boy and his uncle.

Part B

Which sentences from the passages best support your answer in Part A?

    E. "It was Take Your Daughter to Work Day, and I was spending the day with Mom at her office." ("Priya at the Office"); "With each passing birthday, Robert spent more time out on the farm with his father." ("A Different Path")

    F. "'Priya, where are you?' Mom called down the hallway." ("Priya at the Office"); "'What work would you rather be doing right now?'" ("A Different Path")

    G. "There were notes from men, women, children, and coworkers." ("Priya at the Office"); "Then he said, 'Let us take a carriage ride, son.'" ("A Different Path")

    H. "More than one person wrote about how Mom helped to improve their health—and their life in the process." ("Priya at the Office"); "Robert could hear the echo of a hammer strike behind the door." ("A Different Path")

Name_____ Date_____

4. Choose **two** statements that describe a similarity between Priya and Robert.

   A. The character discovered an activity that interests him or her.

   B. The character repaired a troubled relationship with a parent.

   C. The character learned something new about his or her parent.

   D. The character changed from unhappy to happy over the course of the story.

   E. The character made a decision to please a parent rather than him- or herself.

   F. The character enjoyed a situation turning out better than he or she thought it would.

5. Read the sentences from "Priya at the Office."

   > Mom and I arrived at the office at 8:30 a.m., and she began seeing patients promptly at 9 a.m. I wasn't invited into the exam rooms, but I watched the people as they shuffled in and out for their appointments. As the day continued, I was astonished at the significant role my mother played in people's lives!

   Based on these sentences, what is **most likely** true about Priya's mom?

   A. She works as a medical doctor.

   B. She works as a university professor.

   C. She wants Priya to work at her office someday.

   D. She wants Priya to see how important her work is.

6. Compare and contrast the characters' language in the dialogue of "Priya at the Office" and "A Different Path." Use examples from both passages to support your response.

   _____

   _____

   _____

7. Choose **two** statements that are supported by "Priya at the Office" and "A Different Path."

   A. Priya decides to do the same work as her mom, but Robert is not interested in running a farm like his father does.

   B. Priya learns to appreciate her mother's work, but Robert does not change his opinion of farming.

   C. Both Priya and Robert come to understand that in the future they want to do work that helps people.

   D. Priya wants to spend time with her mother at work, but Robert does not want to work with his father.

   E. Both Priya and Robert learn that their parents' work is more challenging than they thought.

   F. Both Priya and Robert were surprised by the results of their experiences that day.

8. This question has two parts.

First answer Part A. Then answer Part B.

Part A

In paragraph 3 of "A Different Path," what is the meaning of the word "dissatisfaction?"

   A. failure to improve

   B. struggle to keep up

   C. confusion in learning

   D. unhappiness about a situation

Part B

Which sentence from the passage **best** supports your answer in Part A?

   E. "'Where are your thoughts, son?' Father's voice disturbed Robert's daydream."

   F. "He was teaching Robert how to determine when the harvest was ready."

   G. "Robert answered quickly, 'I am listening, Father,' but Father had noticed his son's dissatisfaction for weeks now."

   H. "'You might not enjoy learning how to manage the farm, but this is important work,' Father explained."

Sea Rose

By H. D.

Rose, harsh rose,
marred and with stint of petals,
meagre flower, thin,
sparse of leaf.

5   more precious
than a wet rose,
single on a stem—
you are caught in the drift.

Stunted, with small leaf,
10 you are flung on the sands,
you are lifted
in the crisp sand
that drives in the wind.

Can the spice-rose
15 drip such acrid fragrance
hardened in a leaf?

The Lily

By William Blake

The modest Rose puts forth a thorn,

The humble sheep a threat'ning horn:

While the Lily white shall in love delight,

Nor a thorn nor a threat stain her beauty bright.

Name_____ Date_____

Compare/Contrast Poetry

REVIEW THE SKILL

To compare and contrast poetry, we consider the same feature in each poem, such as speaker or theme, and we identify the similarities and differences in how the poems treat that feature.

 Home-School Connection

Help your child practice comparing and contrasting by guiding them in a discussion comparing and contrasting aspects of two familiar songs. Lead them by sharing your ideas aloud and by prompting them with questions about how the songs are similar and different.

SAMPLE QUESTION

Explain one way the subject of each poem is similar and one way each is different. Use details from both poems to support your response.

SAMPLE STUDENT ANSWER

In both "Sea Rose" and "The Lily," the subject of the poem is a flower. However, in "Sea Rose," the speaker is talking about one particular flower. It is addressed as "you" in lines 8, 10, and 11. But in "The Lily," the speaker is talking about lilies in general. It is described as "the Lily white."

CLUE 1: Each poem's title clearly identifies its subject. These titles are clues that readers can compare to see that both poems are about a flower.

CLUE 2: In line 8, the speaker in "Sea Rose" does not address a sea rose directly but rather says "you" and describes all sea roses in general.

Now refer to "Sea Rose" and "The Lily" to answer the following questions.

1. Explain two ways that the form of "Sea Rose" is different from the form of "The Lily." Consider the number and length of lines, as well as any patterns of rhythm or rhyme. Use details from both poems to support your response.

_____

_____

2. Read the lines from "Sea Rose."

> "Rose, harsh rose, / marred and with stint of petals, / meagre flower, thin, / sparse of leaf."

Which statement **best** describes the speaker's attitude toward the sea rose, as revealed in these lines?

A. The speaker thinks that the sea rose is an unattractive flower.

B. The speaker feels concern for the state of the sea rose.

C. The speaker finds the sea rose to be depressing.

D. The speaker admires the strength of the sea rose.

3. This question has two parts.

First answer Part A. Then answer Part B.

Part A

In line 9 of "Sea Rose," what is the meaning of the word "stunted?"

A. ancient

B. familiar

C. undersized

D. weightless

Part B

Which phrase from the poem **best** supports your answer in Part A?

E. "small leaf"

F. "crisp sand"

G. "drives in the wind"

H. "flung on the sands"

4. Read the line from "The Lily."

"Nor a thorn nor a threat stain her beauty bright."

Which of these lines from "Sea Rose" presents an idea about its subject that is in direct contrast with the idea presented in the line above?

A. line 2 ("marred and with stint of petals,")

B. line 7 ("single on a stem—")

C. line 10 ("you are flung on the sands,")

D. line 16 ("hardened in a leaf?")

5. Select **two** themes that are addressed in both poems.

A. duty versus honor

B. the value of beauty

C. flawed versus perfect

D. surviving against the odds

E. the power of telling the truth

F. protecting those who cannot protect themselves

6. Read the lines from "The Lily." Then answer the question.

"While the Lily white shall in love delight,"

"Nor a thorn nor a threat stain her beauty bright."

What is the meaning of the word "stain" in this sentence?

A. attract

B. damage

C. decorate

D. warn

7. This question has two parts.

First answer Part A. Then answer Part B.

Part A

Which statement **best** describes a similarity between "Sea Rose" and "The Lily" in how each poem accomplishes its goal?

   A. Both "Sea Rose" and "The Lily" give details of setting to show how their subject is affected by its surroundings.

   B. Both "Sea Rose" and "The Lily" use rhyme to place emphasis on lines that strongly support their main idea.

   C. Both "Sea Rose" and "The Lily" compare their subjects to another object to illustrate their main ideas.

   D. Both "Sea Rose" and "The Lily" use simile to describe how their subject is like another object.

Part B

Which pair of lines from the poems **best** supports your answer in Part A?

   E. "Sea Rose" line 3 ("meagre flower, thin,"); "The Lily" line 4 ("Nor a thorn nor a threat stain her beauty bright.")

   F. "Sea Rose" line 7 ("single on a stem—"); "The Lily" line 3 ("While the Lily white shall in love delight,")

   G. "Sea Rose" line 13 ("that drives in the wind."); "The Lily" line 2 ("The humble sheep a threat'ning horn:")

   H. "Sea Rose" line 14 ("Can the spice-rose"); "The Lily" line 1 ("The modest Rose puts forth a thorn,")

8. How is the speaker's point of view in "The Lily" **different** from that of the speaker in "Sea Rose"? Use details from both poems to support your response.

_____

_____

_____

Beach Birthday

By Danielle Martin

Characters

PAPA   *MAMA*

LUISA   *MATEO*

ACT I

1   **Scene.** *Kitchen of a small vacation beach bungalow. PAPA, MAMA, and LUISA sit at the table eating breakfast. Rumbles of thunder are heard in the background.*

2   LUISA (*anxiously*): Oh, no! Our plans are ruined!

3   MAMA: Today's weather is unexpected, but our day isn't ruined. We just have to think of a new plan.

4   PAPA: It is still Mateo's birthday, rain or shine.

5   LUISA: I know, Papa, but we planned to celebrate Mateo's birthday on the beach. He loves the beach!

6   PAPA: Then Mama is right: It's time to think of a new plan.

7   *MATEO enters the room.*

8   MAMA (*enthusiastically*): Happy birthday, my son!

9   PAPA and LUISA (*together*): Happy birthday, Mateo!

10 MATEO: What new plan were you talking about?

11 *PAPA, MAMA, and LUISA look at each other but do not speak.*

12 MAMA (*sighs aloud*): Well, Mateo, we had planned a beach birthday party for you, but it is supposed to rain all day.

13 LUISA (*sadly*): We were going to put the tent up, cook hamburgers on the grill, and play games.

14 MATEO (*enthusiastically*): That sounds fun! Why can't we just move the celebration inside?

15 **Scene 2.** *Living room of small vacation beach bungalow. Scene opens to MAMA, MATEO, and LUISA lounging under a blanket fort playing cards. PAPA carries a pizza box toward them from the door.*

16 PAPA: Dinner is served!

17 MAMA: Excellent! We have pizza, a tent, games, and cake.

18 LUISA: Is there anything else that would make today a great birthday, Mateo?

19 MATEO (*grinning*): No. I have everything I need!

Traffic Jam Stories

By Danielle Martin

Characters

CLARA

UNCLE ARMAND

MOM

LOLA (CLARA's grandmother)

ACT I

1   **Scene.** *Interior of a car. MOM is driving. UNCLE ARMAND is in the passenger seat. CLARA and LOLA sit in the back seat.*

2   CLARA (*impatiently*): How long until we reach the Castillo Family Reunion, Mom?

3   MOM: It's hard to know! This traffic jam is slowing us down.

4   LOLA (*patting CLARA's hand*): I'm sorry you had to miss your friend's party today, Clara.

5   CLARA (*hiding her disappointment*): It's okay, Grandma.

6   UNCLE ARMAND (*to LOLA):* But doesn't this remind you of the traffic we used to have when we first immigrated to the city?

7   CLARA (*surprised*): I never knew you used to live in the city!

8   LOLA: Yes. After I married your Grandpa, we moved from the Philippines to the United States. We lived in the city.

9   MOM (*to LOLA*): Tell Clara about the time you and Grandpa almost met Elvis Presley!

10 LOLA (*laughing*): I had nearly forgotten! Well, when Grandpa played in his band, we went…

11 CLARA (*interrupting her grandmother*): Grandpa was in a BAND?!

12 UNCLE ARMAND: Yes, he was. Grandpa was an excellent guitarist! (*to MOM*) Do you remember when he sang us lullabies with his guitar?

13 MOM (*smiling tenderly*): Oh, yes. Those are some of my favorite memories.

14 *CLARA watches her mother and uncle for a moment, imagining them as children her age. LOLA breaks the silence.*

15 LOLA: Ah! I see that traffic is finally moving well.

16 UNCLE ARMAND: Yes. We'll be at the park in about five minutes.

17 CLARA: Wait, Grandma! You have to explain the story about Grandpa in the band!

18 LOLA (*gathering her things*): I will. Don't forget—we still have the drive home tonight.

19 CLARA (*excitedly*): I know! I can't wait!

REVIEW THE SKILL

To compare and contrast drama, we consider different elements of each play. Then we identify the similarities and differences between these elements.

Home-School Connection

Help your child practice comparing and contrasting by leading them to make connections between favorite movies or television shows. For example, if your child enjoys a movie and a show that are set in different time periods, guide them in discussing how the elements of both are similar and different.

SAMPLE QUESTION

Explain an important difference between the setting of the two plays. Use details from both plays to support your response.

SAMPLE STUDENT ANSWER

The title of each play shares a detail about its setting. The word "beach" in "Beach Birthday" shows that the play is near the ocean. The phrase "traffic jam" in "Traffic Jam Stories" hints that the setting is inside a car. The first set of stage directions for each play clearly identifies what the setting is.

DETAIL 1: Keywords in the titles of the plays show details of the setting before readers even begin reading.

DETAIL 2: Both plays begin with stage directions that give basic information about the setting.

Now refer to "Beach Birthday" and "Traffic Jam Stories" to answer the following questions.

1. What do Mateo from "Beach Birthday" and Clara from "Traffic Jam Stories" have in common? Use details from both plays to support your response.

_____

_____

_____

2. Which word could **best** replace "unexpected" in paragraph 3 of "Beach Birthday"?

   A. inconvenient

   B. peculiar

   C. surprising

   D. unknown

3. This question has two parts.

   First answer Part A. Then answer Part B.

Part A

Which of these inferences is **best** supported by "Beach Birthday"?

   A. Mateo was not upset when his birthday party plans had to change.

   B. Mateo's birthday party was supposed to be a surprise for him.

   C. Mama had planned Mateo's birthday party on her own.

   D. Papa wanted to reschedule the party for the next day.

Part B

Which line from the play **best** supports your answer to Part A?

   E. "MATEO (*enthusiastically*): That sounds fun! Why can't we just move the celebration inside?"

   F. "LUISA (*anxiously*): Oh no! Our plans are ruined!"

   G. "PAPA: Then Mama is right: It's time to think of a new plan."

   H. "MATEO: What new plan were you talking about?"

Name_____ Date_____

4. Choose **three** statements that are **true** about both plays.

    A. The play contains only one act.

    B. The play focuses on one character's experiences.

    C. The play has only one character speaking throughout.

    D. The play contains characters who are family members.

    E. The play shows how characters are affected by the weather.

    F. The play describes how a character acts using stage directions.

5. Which theme is shared by **both** "Beach Birthday" and "Traffic Jam Stories"?

    A. A person can be courageous and cowardly at the same time.

    B. Each of us is in charge of our own happiness.

    C. Life's unexpected changes can lead to fun.

    D. Things are not always as they appear.

6. How is Mateo's experience in "Beach Birthday" different from Clara's experience in "Traffic Jam Stories"? Use details from both plays to support your response.

_____

_____

_____

7. How is the structure of "Beach Birthday" different from the structure of "Traffic Jam Stories"? Use details from both plays to support your response.

_____

_____

_____

8. This question has two parts.

First answer Part A. Then answer Part B.

Part A

Read this sentence from "Traffic Jam Stories."

But doesn't this remind you of the traffic we used to have when we first immigrated to the city?

What is the meaning of the word "immigrated?"
A. to visit a place on vacation
B. to accept support from strangers
C. to help people in another country
D. to move from another country

Part B

Which detail from the play gives a clue to the meaning of "immigrated?"
E. "Yes. After I married your Grandpa, we moved from the Philippines to the United States."
F. "But doesn't this remind you of the traffic we used to have…"
G. "I never knew you used to live in the city!"
H. "This traffic jam is slowing us down."

Unit 1: Discussion Prompts

1. Quoting from the text helped me understand it because …
2. I found it hard to quote the text that …
3. I think this skill is important because …

 AT-HOME ACTIVITIES: *True or False?*

Get a deck of cards. Then, ask your child a question about the unit text. Instruct your child to answer using a quote from the text. Check your child's answer by looking at the text. If your child answered correctly and accurately quoted from the text, your child gets one card. Take turns doing this. Any time you or your child answer incorrectly, remove a card. Ask twenty questions. At the end, the player with the most cards wins.

Unit 2: Discussion Prompts

1. An inference is …
2. Drawing an inference about … helped me understand …
3. I think this skill is important because …

 AT-HOME ACTIVITIES: *Famous Inferences*

Choose a celebrity based on your child's preference. This can be a musician, athlete, scientist, or actor. Then, spend time together viewing or listening to this celebrity. While doing this, ask your child to identify an inference the celebrity made, explain how it is an inference, and identify any details the celebrity gave to support the inference.

Unit 3: Discussion Prompts

1. One question I have about theme is …
2. In my own words, "theme" is …
3. Identifying the theme helps me because …

 AT-HOME ACTIVITIES: *Theme Change!*

Ask your child to identify the theme of his or her favorite story from a book or movie. Then, take turns suggesting one change in the story and how that would affect the theme. Take turns identifying stories, suggesting a change, and then discussing how the change would affect the theme.

Unit 4: Discussion Prompts

1. In general, the unit text was about …
2. The most important details were …
3. Summarizing what I read is helpful because …

 AT-HOME ACTIVITIES: *Snip-Glue-Summary*

Photocopy a story your child enjoys. Instruct your child to cut out important details from the story. Then help your child use the important details to craft a summary by gluing the words onto a new piece of paper. Encourage your child to write words that are needed to complete the summary.

Unit 5: Discussion Prompts

1. When I picture the character in my head, I imagine this character …

2. The setting reminds me of a time when …

3. Describing events helps me …

 AT-HOME ACTIVITIES: *Book Charades*

Encourage your child to silently act out different scenes from different books. Explain to your child that the scenes can depict a character, a place or setting, or an event from any of the stories. As your child silently acts out his or her scene, make guesses about the character, scene, or event your child is acting out.

Unit 6: Discussion Prompts

1. It was … to think about how characters are alike.

2. It was … to think about how characters are different.

3. This skill helped me …

 AT-HOME ACTIVITIES: *I Wake Up Transformed Into?*

Help your child write a story about waking up and being transformed into someone else. Encourage him or her to include details about how being this other person is similar or different. Ask your child how living a day in the life of this other person would be similar or different from his or her own life.

Unit 7: Discussion Prompts

1. It was … to think about how settings are alike.

2. It was … to think about how settings are different.

3. This skill helped me …

 AT-HOME ACTIVITIES: *My Dream Trips*

Make a travel brochure with your child. Your child can draw pictures or use magazine clippings to portray places he or she would like to visit, and then write a description of each place. When your child is done, staple the pages together to form a brochure. Discuss with your child how the places are similar or different.

Unit 8: Discussion Prompts

1. Thinking about how events are alike made me realize …

2. Thinking about how events are different made me realize …

3. This skill helped me …

 AT-HOME ACTIVITIES: *Zany Tales*

Ask your child to randomly name a place, a person, and a time (past, present, or future). Then ask your child to retell a familiar story (such as a fairy tale) using these details. Discuss how the events in the story are similar and different between the original and your child's retelling.

Unit 9: Discussion Prompts

1. Some science words I found were …
2. When I read and find a confusing word, I can …
3. Figuring out the meaning of words helped me …

 AT-HOME ACTIVITIES: *Guess My Sketch*

Ask your child to identify unfamiliar words from the unit text. Next, draw a picture of what the word means. Keep drawing clues until your child correctly guesses the meaning of the word. Reread the sentence in which the word occurs in the story. Discuss its meaning.

Unit 10: Discussion Prompts

1. A simile is …
2. One simile from the unit text was …
3. Understanding similes helped me …

 AT-HOME ACTIVITIES: *Wild Similes*

Ask your child to write five similes that are as zany or unlikely as possible. But tell your child to make sure the similes do compare two things using "like" or "as." Then discuss the similes together.

Unit 11: Discussion Prompts

1. A metaphor is …

2. One metaphor from the unit text was …

3. Understanding metaphors helped me …

 AT-HOME ACTIVITIES: *Metaphors in Music*

With your child, listen to music that has lyrics. Anytime either of you hear a metaphor, stop the music and discuss. What was the metaphor? What two things were compared?

Unit 12: Discussion Prompts

1. A chapter is …

2. A stanza is …

3. A scene is …

 AT-HOME ACTIVITIES: *Video Class*

Tell your child to "be the teacher" and teach the parts of texts, including chapters, stanzas, and scenes. Help your child prepare the materials and the presentation he or she will give. Either have your child give the presentation to a group of friends and family, or video record your child's presentation. Then, watch it together and discuss.

Unit 13: Discussion Prompts

1. When the character did ..., it made ... happen.
2. When ... happened in the story, I felt ...
3. Describing how texts build helps me ...

 AT-HOME ACTIVITIES: *Domino Effect*

Ask your child to identify how the main character's actions in the unit text caused the story to happen. Write down the actions from the story that your child tells you. Then work with your child to line up dominoes to represent each action. Push the first domino and watch the "story unfold" as the other dominoes fall.

Unit 14: Discussion Prompts

1. One type of narrator is ...
2. Narrators and speakers use words like ...
3. This unit helped me ...

 AT-HOME ACTIVITIES: *Be the Narrator*

Pick an activity your child enjoys. Ask your child to tell a story about other children doing this activity using "he" and "she." Explain that this is a third person narrator. Then ask your child to tell a story in which he or she does the activity using "I." Explain that this is a first person narrator.

Unit 15: Discussion Prompts

1. This word/description shows a belief of …

2. This word/description shows an opinion of …

3. This word/description shows a feeling of …

 AT-HOME ACTIVITIES: *A New Point of View*

Make masks with your child with craft supplies. Instruct your child to make a different mask to represent different points of view, such as negative, happy, envious, and so on. Then, with your child, try on the masks and walk around your house. Ask your child to describe what he or she sees when wearing each mask and taking on its point of view.

Unit 16: Discussion Prompts

1. The illustrations showed me that the characters …

2. I figured out that … would happen next based on the illustration …

3. Using details in illustrations helped me …

 AT-HOME ACTIVITIES: *Let's Look at the Pictures*

Pick a book with illustrations. Look over all the illustrations with your child, but cover up the words with your hands. Then read the book. Talk about what you and your child understood just by looking at the illustrations and then from reading the book.

Unit 17: Discussion Prompts

1. Some types of multimedia are …
2. The kind of multimedia I like the best are …
3. Using multimedia helped me …

 AT-HOME ACTIVITIES: *Be the Movie Critic*

There are many books that have been made into movies. Identify a book that your child has read but has not yet seen the movie version of. Discuss the book with your child, then watch the movie together. Ask your child how the movie influenced his or her opinion and understanding of the story.

Unit 18: Discussion Prompts

1. The themes, characters, plot, or setting of the stories were …
2. These stories were more alike/different in that …
3. Comparing and contrasting helped me …

 AT-HOME ACTIVITIES: *Venn Diagram*

Work with your child to create a Venn diagram. Ask your child to draw a circle for different stories he or she has read, using a different color marker. Your child should have circles overlap to show stories that are similar. Tell your child to write each part of the story that is unique or different within a circle, and then write parts that are similar within the overlapping spaces.

Unit 19: Discussion Prompts

1. The themes, characters, or settings of the poems were …

2. These poems were more alike/different in that …

3. Comparing and contrasting helped me …

 AT-HOME ACTIVITIES: *Poetry Scavenger Hunt*

With your child, develop a list of five ways poems could be alike and five ways poems could be different. Then, bring your child to a library or bookstore. Encourage your child to find poems that fulfill all ten things listed.

Unit 20: Discussion Prompts

1. The themes, characters, plot, or setting of the dramas were …

2. These dramas were more alike/different in that …

3. Comparing and contrasting helped me …

 AT-HOME ACTIVITIES: *The Movie and Drama Game*

Identify a trait—such as a theme, characteristic, plot, or setting—and ask your child to name as many movies or plays as possible that contain this trait. When your child is "stumped" and unable to name another, switch and have your child name a trait in order for you to name movies.

Answer Key

Unit 1

pages 14–17

1. Sample answer: In the second sentence, the narrator says, "there's something you should probably know: I'm deaf." Because he cannot hear, his teachers might be worried he might not be able to sail safely alone. They might feel this is too dangerous for someone who is deaf.

2. **B, E** In the fifth paragraph, the text states, "I had to climb on top of the boat and carefully push the far end of the boat until the mast came out of the water." These details explain the steps he needed to take to right his boat.

3. **D** A "destination" is a place someone is going to. In this sentence, the narrator's destination is "an island owned by my sailing school."

4. The quotes go in the following order: (1) **B** "my parents stuck up for me." (2) **E** "The ocean spread out before me like a clean sheet across my bed." (3) **D** "Soon, though, a dark cloud loomed on the horizon." (4) **C** "my boat capsized, and waves covered my head" (5) **A** "I finally flipped the boat."

5. **Part A**   **B**

   Part B   **E, G**   The narrator is ready to sail to the island alone. This idea is supported by the fact that he "knew what to do" when the weather changed and his boat capsized and that he had sailed in storms before and therefore knew how to read the wind.

6. Sample answer: In the story, the narrator says that he "knew to pay attention to every tiny detail," including watching telltales. When the wind knocks him down and capsizes his boat, he knew "what to do." He says, "I had to climb on top of the boat and carefully push the far end of the boat until the mast came out of the water." He doesn't panic. Instead, he fixes his problem. His parents must have known that he had these kinds of skills and abilities. They make him a great sailor.

Unit 2

pages 18–21

1. Sample answer: In the third paragraph, Louisa says, "It was in this little velvet bag at the bottom of your jewelry box, just like everything else in there." If the ring was with everything else, there would be no indication that Louisa couldn't play with it along with all the other jewelry. So she could rightly be confused.

2. **B, D** From the way that Grandma grabs the ring, puts it in her pocket, and walks away, the most reasonable inferences would be that she has a strong emotional attachment to the ring and that she doesn't want to talk about it.

3. **B** Based on the context clues, the meaning of "stumbled" in this sentence is "to make mistakes or hesitate in speech."

Answer Key

4. Sample answer: Since Grandma was upset about Bébé Or and left the room, I can make the inference that she doesn't want to talk about it. Louisa knows this, and so she knows she will have to find out about the ring on her own. She can assume that Grandma would not want her to try to find out more about the ring, since she seemed so angry just that Louisa was wearing it. That's why Louisa has to sneak up to the attic.

5. **Part A**   **B**

   Part B   **G**   The most reasonable inference is that Louisa had never heard Grandma talk about her husband because he went to fight in the Korean War and died during his service. It is most reasonable to assume that Louisa didn't know much, or anything, about her grandfather.

6. Sample answer: Based on their conversation at the end of the story, I think that their relationship is strong and positive. Louisa eventually got Grandma to open up about her past and the ring's importance to her. This tells me that they have an honest and close relationship overall.

Unit 3
pages 22–25

1. Sample answer: From reading the poem's title, a reader can see the two characters that the poem will be about. Even before I read the poem, I can guess that it will be about the relationship between the lion and the hunter and maybe how they affect each other.

2. **A** "Tremendous," as used here, means "enormous in size and power."

3. **A, C, D**   The speaker talks about blood pumping through muscles, the lion being tremendous and fearsome, and the great creature's color being tawny. These are positive characteristics of a living lion, and they support the theme that wild animals should be allowed to remain free, beautiful, powerful, and alive.

4. Sample answer: The speaker pictures the hunter "kneeling over the lion," as if he is superior to the lion. The speaker also says that the hunter "smiles a grin like a sneer," which makes it seem like he is mocking or making fun of the lion. These descriptions do not create a positive picture of the hunter, and so I think the speaker disapproves of the hunter and what he's done.

Answer Key

5. Part A   B

Part B   H   Based on the text, the speaker believes that the hunter stole something amazing and beautiful from the world and ruined it. By using the phrase, "There is no glory here," the speaker shares a clear opinion about the hunter killing the lion. This detail is important for understanding the overall theme.

6. Sample answer: The theme of the poem is letting living creatures be wild and free. Even though the hunter thought that killing and mounting the lion was a victory for him, he has made the world a worse place by removing a magnificent animal from it. The theme is about leaving wild animals alone instead of trying to kill them to keep as personal prizes.

Unit 4

pages 26–29

1. Sample answer: The narrator's brother, while eating breakfast, tells her that he no longer wants to share a room with her. He says the arrangement is too childish.

2. A, E Although all of these details appear in the paragraphs, the two details explaining how Christiane feels about moving out of her room are best to include in a summary. They are the most important details in the paragraphs.

3. A "Stunned," in this context, means "extremely surprised."

4. The order of events is as follows: (1) **D** Robert decides that he and Christiane need to have separate rooms. (2) **C** Mom suggests that they turn the guest room into Christiane's room. (3) **B** Christiane ignores Robert's explanation and gets ready for school in silence. (4) **A** Christiane notices the similarity between doing the splits and her brother's idea. (5) **E** Christiane offers to help Robert paint his new room.

5. Part A   C

Part B   E   While Christiane is practicing gymnastics, she sees the parallel between a physically difficult move (the splits) and the emotional difficulty of moving out of her room. She realizes, "It's going to hurt at first, but then I'll get used to it." She recognizes that in the new arrangement they'll both have extra room to stretch out.

6. Sample answer: Christiane's brother decides that he wants to end their shared bedroom arrangement. Christiane is stunned and heartbroken, even when her brother says that it doesn't change the way he feels about her. Later, while practicing gymnastics, Christiane is doing splits, which can be painful and challenging. She realizes that the two situations are similar in that they might be painful at first, but they also allow for growth. She decides to support Robert's decision and embrace the change.

Answer Key

Unit 5

pages 30–33

1. Sample answer: Near the beginning, the text says that Bear went "lumbering down to the lake," so we learn that the story takes place at a lake. The text also says it is a "chilly day," and that Fox was "relaxing on the ice." These details tell us that it is cold and that the lake is frozen, so the story must take place during the winter.

2. D, E The question asks for specific happenings that are part of Fox's big plan to trick Bear. In the fourth paragraph, Fox tells Bear "to drop his tail into the water," and in the sixth paragraph, Fox sneaks up "on the sleeping bear." These details from the text support answer choices D and E.

3. C The question asks the meaning of the word "furious" in this specific context. Here, the word "furious" means "extremely angry," which is answer choice C. The use of the word "but" tells us that Fox's giggling is different from Bear being "furious" and helps us determine the meaning of the term.

4. D This question addresses Bear's character, and asks why he felt as confident as he did. In the fifth paragraph, the text states that "Because Bear was so vain about his tail, he was confident that he could catch more fish than any other animal could." The detail about Bear's vanity supports answer choice D.

5. Part A   A

   Part B   H   This question addresses Fox's character, asking why she was giggling. Fox was giggling because she was pleased that she had tricked Bear and taught him a lesson for being so vain about his tail. Therefore answer choice A in Part A is correct. The reader can infer this because the text states that "Everyone thought Bear was very vain" and that Fox had therefore decided to trick him in order to teach him a lesson. Answer choice H in Part B reflects this information.

6. Sample answer: Bear was vain and "loved to show off" his long, beautiful tail. Fox was tricky, and she wanted to teach Bear a lesson. The interactions between these two characters move the story forward. We know from clues in the text, such as Fox "relaxing on the ice," that the setting is on a lake during winter. If it hadn't been on a lake during winter, Fox's trick never would have worked. All the parts of the story help make the story make sense.

Answer Key

Unit 6

pages 34–37

1. Sample answer: Peter Pan is in this room because he is looking for his shadow there. Peter asks Tinker Bell if she knows "where they put" his shadow, and "Tink said that the shadow was in the big box." Then Peter pulls everything out of the chest of drawers, "scattering their contents," and we can guess he is looking for his shadow. He finds it and tries to reattach it, even trying "to stick it on with soap from the bathroom." This seems like the reason Peter came into this room.

2. **B** The question asks for a description of Tinker Bell's language, which is an important part of her character that makes her different from Peter Pan. The text reads, "The loveliest tinkle as of golden bells answered him. It is the fairy language." This text supports answer choice B.

3. **D, E** The question asks for ways that Peter Pan and Tinker Bell are different. The reader can infer that both are interested in finding Peter Pan's shadow, because "Tink said that the shadow was in the big box." The reader can infer that both characters entered the room through the window, since Peter Pan "had carried Tinker Bell part of the way" there. But Peter Pan can be understood by ordinary people, such as Wendy, unlike Tinker Bell. Peter Pan can carry Tinker Bell in his hand, so that he is much bigger than her.

4. **C** Using context clues, the reader can see that the word can't mean "lost," because Peter Pan wouldn't feel "delight" if he had lost his shadow again. He didn't remember his shadow, because this also would not cause "delight." And he took everything out of the drawers to find his shadow, so it wouldn't make sense for the shadow to be covered up. Therefore the correct answer choice must be C.

5. **Part A**   **C**

   Part B   **H**   The question asks for information about Peter Pan's character, particularly how he behaves toward Tinker Bell. The text shows that Peter Pan doesn't thank her for finding his shadow, which is a rude and thoughtless way to treat one's friend, and so the correct answer in Part A is C. Part B asks which detail gives the best evidence for Peter Pan's self-centeredness. The fact that he "forgot that he had shut Tinker Bell up in the drawer" is the clearest evidence of this. So the best answer in Part B is H.

Answer Key

6. Sample answer: According to the text, Peter Pan and Tinker Bell are both a little silly. Tinker Bell spends time in a jug, "liking it extremely," and Peter somehow gets separated from his shadow. They both also understand the fairy language, and so we know they're not regular people. Peter and Tinker Bell are different because: Peter is a boy and Tinker Bell is girl; Peter is bigger than Tinker Bell and "carried Tinker Bell part of the way"; Peter seems self-centered and not particularly nice while Tinker Bell seems helpful; and Peter can be understood by regular people while Tinker Bell can't be understood by everyone.

Unit 7

pages 38–41

1. Sample answer: This paragraph says that Earth had become too polluted and that the air had become painful to breathe. It says that the planet had become too hot and that the weather had changed so quickly that the trees lost their leaves. This all helps explain why the planet is becoming uninhabitable.

2. **C, E** In the third paragraph the text states, "There were lakes, but only in perfect circles" and "Trees had no branches—they stood straight up and down like telephone poles." These are two traits that make Nova Loko different from Earth.

3. **D** A "survey" is an official close examination of something to see what value it has. In this case, it is a survey of planets that might be inhabitable.

4. **D** In the third paragraph, the text states that Nova Loko was "a safe distance from a sun." We know that Earth is also a safe distance from our sun, thus this is the correct answer.

5. **Part A**   **D**

   Part B   **F**   Bea is referring to her impending move to a new setting—that of Nova Loko. She is deciding to accept the change and embrace the move to the new planet. The text says she thinks that it is time for something new, as difficult and scary as it might be. This indicates that she's planning to accept the change and decide to be happy about it.

6. Sample answer: Both Earth and Nova Loko are planets that people can live on. They are both a safe distance from a sun. But Earth's air is no longer healthy. Nova Loko, on the other hand, has healthy air, and it is a safe place to live. It has lakes, like Earth, but they are only in perfect circles. It has trees, like Earth, but its trees have no branches. Unlike Earth, Nova Loko has a green sky and red stems covering the ground. Bea understands that moving from Earth to Nova Loko is important, even though it is scary, because it's a healthier place to live than Earth. She accepts the change and the move.

Conquer New Standards: Literary Text • Grade 5 • © Newmark Learning, LLC

Answer Key

Unit 8

pages 42–45

1. Sample answer: The first two races were the same as the second two because they were all competitions with other runners and Yusef finished them all. The first two were different from the next two, though, because he won the first two easily and he struggled in the second two. The first paragraph describes how easily Yusef won the first two races. The second paragraph says, "In his third and fourth races, Yusef struggled to keep up with the winners."

2. **B, D** The text explains that Yusef struggled to keep up with the winning runners in the third and fourth races. It states that he placed third in his fourth race only because a boy in front of him sprained his ankle. These are events that led to Yusef doubting his abilities and talents.

3. **C** Based on the context clues, the meaning of "stride" in the story is "a regular pace while running or walking."

4. Sample answer: During both conversations, Yusef's coach told Yusef that she thought he could be the "best" or "fastest" distance runner in town. The conversations were similar in this way. In the second conversation, though, Yusef told Coach Margaret that he wanted to quit. She told him, "You can quit if you want to." But she also said she still believed he could be great, if he was "willing to work at it." She let him know she thought he should keep trying.

5. **Part A**   **B**

   Part B   **H**   After listening to his coach, Yusef decided that he would work harder to get better at running. To do this, he started lifting weights with his legs and practicing to improve his technique right away.

6. Sample answer: Yusef began the season feeling "unbeatable," especially after he won his first two races easily. But when he lost his second two races, he felt discouraged. As the text states, he felt "maybe he wasn't as talented as he had thought." He even wanted to quit running. But his coach told him that she believed in him. This conversation helped Yusef make an important decision. He decided to work harder, and because of this he was able to win his last race. He became a stronger and more confident person.

Answer Key

Unit 9

pages 46–49

1. Sample answer: The word "captivated" in this story means "very interested." The king liked the idea of having "the finest clothes in the land." His response to the report was to act "quickly" and to have the strangers start work "immediately." This shows that he was interested and eager after hearing what the strangers had told him.

2. Sample answer: "Tailors" are people whose job it is to make clothes. The king hires them "to make clothing for him." The story tells that the king likes to have "the finest clothes," so it makes sense that he would hire people who specialize in making clothes.

3. **C, E** Answer choices C and E both tell the reader that there were no clothes made. The strangers only "pretended to weave" clothes and the king eventually "realized he had been duped."

4. **B** In this story, the word "duped" seems to mean "tricked." When the king realizes an "innocent young boy" sees nothing, just as the king saw nothing, he understands how the three strangers tricked him into not believing his own eyes.

5. **B** In this story, the strangers claim they can "fashion a set of clothes" from a special cloth. The story then says they "got to work" and "pretended to weave" the clothes, so "fashion" must mean "make."

6. **Part A**   **C**

   Part B   **G**   Answer choice C shows the most likely meaning of the word "competent." The king is said to be happy that he would be able to tell who was "smart and trustworthy at their jobs."

Unit 10

pages 50–53

1. Sample answer: The first line, which is also the title of the poem, is a simile. The poem compares an emerald to grass. It uses the words "is as green as" to show that emeralds are similar to grass because they are both green.

2. **A** The word "fair" is used in this poem to mean "beautiful." When the speaker says "As fair art thou" (meaning as "As fair as you"), he is speaking to the woman he loves. He has already described her as being like a new rose and a sweet song, so we can infer that, here, he means that she is as beautiful as a flower or a song. These lines of the poem can be read as "As beautiful as you are, that is how much in love I am."

3. **A, F** Answer choices A and F are examples of similes because they both compare one object to a different object, using the word "as." The speaker compares "A ruby" to "blood" by saying the ruby is "red as blood." The speaker compares the way a "sapphire shines" to "heaven" by saying the sapphire "shines as blue as heaven."

Conquer New Standards: Literary Text • Grade 5 • © Newmark Learning, LLC

Answer Key

4. Sample answer: The author of "An Emerald Is As Green As Grass" used similes to describe how interesting the colors of different gems are. The descriptions "An emerald is as green as grass" and a ruby is "red as blood" both show readers in vivid ways how these stones look. These are both similes because they use "as" to show comparisons.

5. **Part A   C**

   Part B   G   The author of "An Emerald Is As Green As Grass" most likely used this simile as a way to contrast sapphires with flint. The next line describes a flint, stating, "A flint lies in the mud." This shows a contrast to the line about sapphires. Additionally, the end of the poem mentions a flint again. In reading the entire poem, we see it is meant to show that stones like emeralds and sapphires may be beautiful and flint may not be beautiful, but flint is still very important.

6. Sample answer: The author of "A Red, Red Rose" wrote "O my Luve's like the melodie, / That's sweetly play'd in tune." I know this is a simile because of the words "like the" before the word "melodie." I think the word "melodie" is the same as "melody" because he says it is "sweetly play'd in tune." This simile tells us that the speaker's "Luve" is similar to a sweet melody, which means that she is very sweet and lovely.

Unit 11
pages 54–57

1. Sample answer: The line "Orpheus's voice was a spoonful of honey" is a metaphor used to describe Orpheus's singing. It's a metaphor because it states that his voice was something else, not just that it was "like" something else. Orpheus's voice was not actually a spoonful of honey. The metaphor is used to show that Orpheus had a very pleasing voice.

2. **C, E** The question asks readers to find more metaphors in the passage. Answer choices C and E are examples of metaphors because they describe one thing by naming it as a different thing.

3. Sample answer: This metaphor compares Orpheus's path out of Hades to a tightrope. The metaphor means that Orpheus walked very straight and very carefully, just like a performer on a tightrope. He did not actually walk on a tightrope but walked carefully so he would not turn or stumble. The text says he "did not move left or right but looked down in front of his feet the entire way."

4. **C** The question asks readers to define the word "stern" as it is used in the passage. In this context, the word "stern" means "tough and strict." Pluto is described as having a heart that is a "stone wall" and as never letting "a loved one return to the world of the living." These details tell the reader that Pluto was not someone who was easy to bargain with.

Answer Key

5. Sample answer: This metaphor means that Orpheus and Eurydice were both so in love with each other that nothing could break them up. When Eurydice was bitten by a snake and died, Orpheus felt so "empty" that he went to the world of the dead to get her back. And his song about his love for her was so meaningful that it affected even Pluto, whose "hard heart was moved."

6. Part A   **B**

    Part B   **H**   This question addresses a metaphor about Pluto. In Part A, answer choices A and C do provide descriptions of Pluto, but they do not compare him to something else, or claim he is something else, and therefore they are not metaphors. The statement that his "heart was a stone wall" (answer choice B) is a metaphor that shows Pluto did not have many feelings. In Part B, answer choice H best supports the idea that his "heart was a stone wall" was a metaphor.

Unit 12

pages 58–61

1. Sample answer: The first four stanzas are all about specific seasons and the fruits that are available and fresh during that time. The fifth stanza is the last stanza. This stanza is about fruit in general, and how fruit is great all year round.

2. B The speaker mentions "autumn" and the "sound of crunch" in stanza 3. Stanza 2 is about summer, stanza 4 is about winter, and stanza 5 is a summation of all the previous stanzas. So the answer must be choice B.

3. D, E The first stanza of the poem sets up the structure by pairing a season with a fruit that grows in that season. This supports answer choice D. Also, the poem begins with spring, which is the first season of the year, and then continues stanza-by-stanza through the seasons as they occur sequentially throughout the year. This supports answer choice E.

4. A To figure out the meaning of the word, readers must look at the context. In the line before, the text mentions apples, which are fruit and something that is eaten. They are also crisp and would make a crunching sound when they are bitten into. The poem also mentions a "sound."

5. Part A   **D**

    Part B   **H**   Based on details in stanza 4, eating fruit in the winter is harder than it is in the fall. The fifth stanza says very clearly that it is "going to get tough."

Answer Key

6. Sample answer: Based on the details in the poem, I think the speaker is someone who really likes eating seasonal fruit. The speaker says that fruit's "sweet taste is always a treat!" The speaker even admits that sometimes it is hard to get fruit, but makes it sound like it is worth it.

Unit 13

pages 62–65

1. Sample answer: I think this is a detective story. Nolan comes to Kamilah for help. She explains to the reader that she often helps people, saying that her classmates regard her "as someone who could help" and that she "could get things done and solve problems." She also says she is known as "the 'PI'—private investigator," and that she always does her best to "crack the case." These details tell me that Kamilah is like a detective and that the story will be a detective story.

2. A, D The question asks about the qualities Kamilah notes about Nolan. In the first sentence of the third paragraph, she says that he is the "tallest kid in fifth grade." Next she says that "he didn't say much" and that "this was the first time he had ever approached" her. These details, which help build the story, support answer choices A and D.

3. A To figure out the meaning of "reputation," readers must look at the context. The last two choices don't make a lot of sense based on the context of these sentences. Choice B is more similar to the definition of "reputation," but because the text shows that Kamilah acts on the side of kindness, the reader can infer that she is not known for acting badly. Based on context and details from the text, the correct choice must be A.

4. D The question is addressing a detail about Kamilah that is important for building this detective story. In the fourth paragraph, the text says that Kamilah can "get things done and solve problems." In other paragraphs, the text says that Kamilah doesn't help everyone who asks, and indicates that she would rather not be president because "being president takes up too much free time." The text does not say that she dislikes Nolan. Therefore, evidence from the text supports answer choice D.

5. Part A   D

   Part B   E   As the reader thinks about the question, he or she must suspect that this is not the entire story. The reader can therefore guess that Kamilah would have to take the case in order to keep the story going. Everything the reader has learned so far indicates that she will help Nolan. This idea is supported by the line "I feared it would be a long afternoon"— meaning, Kamilah would probably spend the afternoon helping Nolan.

Answer Key

6. Sample answer: The text shows the beginning of a story. Based on the story so far, we know that Kamilah is someone who can "solve problems." She is willing to spend time figuring things out, and she says that she is "just better at it than most." These details give the reader confidence that she will be able to help Nolan find his dog.

Unit 14

pages 66–69

1. Sample answer: The doctor thinks visiting the Alps will help Clara get better. So the doctor views the Alps as a happy and helpful place. This is supported by details in the passage. For example, Clara writes that the doctor said, "it was so quiet in the pure, delicious air, away from towns and streets, that everybody has to get well there." Clara also writes that the doctor talked a lot about "the mountains and the flowers he saw." This shows how much the doctor enjoyed his time in the Alps.

2. **C** There are context clues in the passage that reveal the meaning of the word "declines." The previous sentence in the passage says "Miss Rottenmeier does not want to go." This shows that when Miss Rottenmeier "declines," she is refusing to go on the trip. Therefore, the word "declines" means "refuses" in the passage.

3. **Part A   C**

Part B   E   Based on the text, the reader can infer that Clara is not well and her doctor thinks the trip will improve her health. The fact that Clara has a doctor shows that she is not well. In the text, the doctor says, "it was so quiet in the pure, delicious air, away from towns and streets, that everybody has to get well there." This shows that Clara is going to the Alps to get better.

4. **E, F** Answer choices E and F show how grandmama feels and thinks. So these details reveal grandmama's point of view, namely that she loves Heidi and that she is happy to be visiting Heidi in the Alps.

5. **B** In the first paragraph, the author says that Heidi went, "bounding over to her grandfather." The word "bounding" means that Heidi was leaping and bouncing. This shows that she was excited about the letter. She also immediately offers to read the letter to her grandfather, which shows that she is excited to read Clara's letter.

Conquer New Standards: Literary Text • Grade 5 • © Newmark Learning, LLC

Answer Key

6. Sample answer: Clara can't wait to visit Heidi in the Alps, while Miss Rottenmeier does not want to go on the trip because she is afraid of heights. Clara's point of view is made clear when she says, "Oh, how I look forward to it all!" when referring to the trip. The reader can determine Miss Rottenmeier's point of view because Clara says that Sebastian gave Miss Rottenmeier "such a terrible description of the high rocks and fearful abysses, that she is afraid." The letter also says that Miss Rottenmeier does not want "to take the risk."

Unit 15

pages 70–73

1. Sample answer: Because the narrator's point of view is third person, the reader can tell that Sara thinks the house was similar to Miss Minchin, who she does not like. Her thoughts and feelings about Miss Minchin shape the way the narrator describes the house. The following sentences from the story describe the house in a negative and stern way: "It was respectable and well furnished, but everything in it was ugly; and the very armchairs seemed to have hard bones in them. In the hall everything was hard and polished—even the red cheeks of the moon face on the tall clock in the corner had a severe varnished look."

2. **A, B** Answer choices A and B both show Sara's feelings or point of view in the story. Sara is nervous and does not like the house. She also doesn't like Miss Minchin.

3. **D** In this context, the word "severe" means "stern." In the sentence, everything is described as having a harsh or serious look, even something that should be happy, like the "red cheeks of the moon face on the tall clock."

4. Sample answer: Captain Crewe loves Sara and is sad to leave her. I made this inference based on the details in the story. For example, the story says, "And then suddenly he swept her into his arms and kissed her very hard." The Captain stopped laughing and looked "as if tears had come into his eyes." This shows how much Captain Crewe loves Sara and is sad to leave her.

5. **Part A   A**

   Part B   H   Captain Crewe wants to hide his sadness from Sara. He acts cheerful and tries to lighten her mood. The sentence, "'Here we are, Sara,' said Captain Crewe, making his voice sound as cheerful as possible," shows that Captain Crewe makes himself sound cheerful for Sara's sake.

6. **C** Answer choice "C" supports the conclusion that Sara's father is leaving to fight.

Answer Key

Unit 16

pages 74–77

1. Sample answer: The "creator" character is angry, but the text does not describe what he is doing. Panel 2 shows him with a fist. By looking at the illustration in panel 2, it is clear that the master is ready to fight.

2. **B** Answer choice B best identifies the mood. The pictures show a man in a lonely place without any people, houses or towns nearby.

3. Sample answer: The illustration in panel 5 shows that the monster is very angry. The monster's face looks angry and he has a fist formed. When he says "The whole world will share in my wretchedness," he doesn't mean that the world will somehow become sad. Panel 5 suggest that he will make people feel wretched by fight everyone in the world. Without the illustration, a reader might think the monster is sad, instead of very angry.

4. **A, D** Answer choices A and D are supported by the illustrations. The monster and Frankenstein have stopped fighting and are walking together toward a small cave with a fire. Since the monster wanted to talk with Frankenstein, I think the monster set up this fire.

5. **A** In this passage, the word "entreat" means to ask or beg. The monster begs Frankenstein to be calm, even though he is much stronger than Frankenstein.

6. **Part A**   **D**

   Part B   **F**   There is nothing in the text that says the monster is larger than Frankenstein. The illustration in panel 4, however, show that the monster is in fact much larger.

Unit 17

pages 78–81

1. Sample answer: When I read the story, I was focused on the details of the conversation, like how Corriston was wounded and how another person was wounded by a "poisonous" "Martian barb." But when I listened to the conversation, I heard more of the characters' personalities, such as how the Captain sounded very commanding and serious, whereas Corriston sounded worried. The story said Corriston had a "voice that trembled a little," but I was more affected when I heard a scared and worried voice.

2. **D** Paragraph 1 states that the wound had "ceased to bleed profusely," and the injury had "severed no more than a superficial ligament." This suggests that the cut was not deep and had not caused serious damage. It only caused minor or slight damage. Therefore, answer choice D is correct.

Answer Key

3. Sample answer: When I read the story silently, I was paying attention to reading words I didn't know as well as trying to understand the story. So I needed to use details and context clues to understand the meaning of the words, such as "ligament" and "mandatory." Also, I needed to think about who was speaking and what they were saying. But when I listened, the person reading used a different tone of voice for each character. This helped me really focus more on what the character's thought and felt.

4. **Part A**   C

   Part B   G   Corriston was most likely injured from being in a fight with someone who had a knife. The text says that "the knife had severed no more than a superficial ligament" and also that Corriston had "tangled" with a man. So these details suggest he had a fight, and the man used a knife as a weapon.

5. **C, E** Answer choices B and D can only be done when reading a text, not while listening to a text read aloud, and answer choices A and F can happen when reading, listening to a text, or looking at illustrations. Only answer choices C and E can happen when listening to a text read aloud.

6. Sample answer: The illustration helped me understand the story, because it showed me the main characters were probably human. It also shows them looking out a space station into space. They are not looking at Earth. This makes me think they might be near Mars, because the text says someone injured a person with "a plant found only on Mars." So the illustration helped me understand the characters and the setting.

Unit 18
pages 82–87

1. Sample answer: A theme explored in both stories is the way things turn out better than one expects them to sometimes. In "Priya at the Office," Priya does not want to miss a fun day at school to spend time at her mother's office. However, by the end of the day, she has learned something new about her mom, and she has had a good time doing so. In "A Different Path," Robert feels hopeless because he does not enjoy learning about farm work. But by the end of the day, he is excited about his future learning a different trade.

2. **C** The target sentence gives a strong context clue in the clause "...that I didn't hear her enter the room behind me." This clue suggests that Priya was paying close attention to the cards she was viewing, or that she was interested in them.

Answer Key

3. **Part A**   **C**

   Part B   **E**   The description of the narrators of each story is the only option that describes a true difference between the two stories. The sentence from "Priya at the Office" shows the narrator's use of the pronoun I, which is a characteristic of a first person narrator. The sentence from "A Different Path" shows the narrator describing characters without using first person pronouns.

4. **D, F** At the beginning of their stories, both Priya and Robert were not happy with how they were spending their time. But by the end of her story, Priya learned a lot about her mom and seemed to enjoy her day. Robert was also happy at the end of his story because he learned that he would learn an interesting trade. Priya did not want to go to her mother's office, and Robert did not want to spend time learning about the farm, but both were pleased with how their day turned out.

5. **A** Such clues as "seeing patients," "exam rooms," and "appointments" support the inference that Priya's mother is a medical doctor.

6. Sample answer: The characters' dialogue in "Priya at the Office" is more relaxed and similar to the way people talk today. One example of this familiar, informal dialogue is Priya's final line: "'Did I hear you say something about ice cream?'" In "A Different Path," the characters speak more formally and in an old-fashioned way. For example, Robert's father tells him, "'Let us take a carriage ride, son.'"

7. **B, F** By the end of the day, Priya realizes how important her mother's work is. Robert, however, still finds farming boring and longs for more interesting tasks. Priya is surprised by her experiences that day because she learned how important a role her mother plays in others' lives. Robert is surprised because his father understands his feelings about farming and actually offers him a more interesting job to try—blacksmithing.

8. **Part A**   **D**

   Part B   **H**   A strong clue to the meaning of "dissatisfaction" comes in the paragraph after it. When Robert's father says, "You might not enjoy…," he is revealing the meaning of "dissatisfaction": "unhappiness about a situation."

Unit 19

pages 88–93

1. Sample answer: At sixteen lines, "Sea Rose" is much longer than "The Lily," which has four lines. However, "The Lily" has a rhyme scheme of *aabb*. The rhyming words "thorn" and "horn" end lines 1 and 2, while the pair "delight/bright" ends lines 3 and 4. "Sea Rose" does not include rhyme.

Answer Key

2. **A** In this first stanza, the speaker describes the rose as "harsh" and "marred," or damaged. In addition, the rose's one flower is described as "meagre" and "thin." Finally, the speaker points out that the sea rose is also "sparse of leaf," or nearly bare.

3. **Part A**   **C**

   Part B   **E**   The previous stanzas describe the sea rose as damaged, with a small flower and few leaves. In addition, after the word "stunted," this line further describes the leaf as "small." These clues taken together lead to the correct answer "undersized."

4. **A** The line from "The Lily" expresses the idea that nothing can "stain" or blemish the lily's beauty. In line 2 of "Sea Rose," the word "marred" means that something has been blemished or damaged. So the fact that the sea rose is "marred" is in contrast with the idea that nothing could "stain" the lily.

5. **B, C** The value of beauty is examined in "Sea Rose" through the speaker's description of the sea rose's ugliness. The value of beauty is examined in "The Lily" through the speaker's claim that the lily's beauty is perfect, unstained, and better than the Rose or the sheep. The theme of flawed versus perfect is explored in "Sea Rose" through the speaker's description of the sea rose as being damaged and scrawny. In "The Lily," this theme is explored as the speaker describes the flaws of the rose and the sheep and then compares these flaws to the perfection of the lily.

6. **B** The speaker describes the subject of the poem as "the Lily white" and discusses "her beauty bright." Then the speaker states that neither "a thorn nor a threat" will stain this beauty. This suggests that staining would affect the lily negatively, making "damage" the best choice.

7. **Part A**   **C**

   Part B   **H**   In line 14 of "Sea Rose," the speaker compares the sea rose to a "spice-rose," or a popular and respected rose. The speaker suggests that, even with its flaws, the sea rose is more "precious" than a popular rose. In line 1 of "The Lily," the speaker describes a flaw of the rose: its thorn. In line 4, the speaker mentions this flaw again but this time to explain that the perfect lily is not stained by such a flaw. Each poem compares its subject to a rose in order to make its point.

8. Sample answer: Both speakers have a flower as their subject, and both speakers comment on the beauty of that subject. The speaker of "Sea Rose" suggests that it is the very details that make it ugly and different from other roses that also make the sea rose better than other roses. The speaker of "The Lily" suggests that the lily is superior to the rose and the sheep because it has no flaws. In other words, the lily is perfect and superior.

Answer Key

Unit 20

pages 94–99

1. Sample answer: In "Beach Birthday," Mateo does not know that his family has planned a birthday party for him, so he is surprised by the celebration his family is planning for him. On the other hand, Clara had planned to go to a friend's party, but she did not attend in order to go to her family reunion.

2. **C** The word "surprising" most accurately reflects the meaning of "unexpected." Mama and Luisa's lines suggest that the family had planned on different weather that day and that they had to change their plans to work with the change in weather.

3. **Part A   B**

    Part B   H   Mateo did not know a party was planned for him. This detail supports the inference that the party was meant to surprise him.

4. **A, D, F**   Choices A, D, and F are true statements supported by both plays. Both plays have one act, contain characters who are family members, and describes characters' actions using stage directions.

5. **C** In "Beach Birthday," Mateo's family races to change the plans for his outdoor birthday party because of unexpected rainy weather. By the end of the play, it appears that Mateo enjoys his new indoor party very much. In "Traffic Jam Stories," Clara has to miss her friend's party in order to go to an event with her family. In addition, she is stuck in the car for a while on the way to the event because of traffic. During this time, she learns some interesting information about her family, and she is excited to learn more on the drive home. Both characters have fun despite a change of plans.

6. Sample answer: One thing that Mateo and Clara have in common is that both characters end up enjoying a day spent with family members. At the end of "Beach Birthday," Mateo says that there is nothing else he needs to have a great birthday. This suggests that he is enjoying his birthday party with his family. At the end of "Traffic Jam Stories," Clara says that she "can't wait" for the drive home so she can hear more stories about her family. This also suggests that she has enjoyed her time with family so far that day.

7. Sample answer: Both plays are presented in one act. However, "Beach Birthday" contains two scenes, whereas "Traffic Jam Stories" only has one scene.

8. **Part A   D**

    Part B   E   "Immigrated" means "moved from another country." The strongest clue to the meaning of "immigrated" comes from paragraph 8 ("we moved from the Philippines to the United States").

Conquer New Standards: Literary Text • Grade 5 • © Newmark Learning, LLC